PROTECT YOURSELF FROM VIRUSES:

Definitive Hand Sanitizer and Medical Face Mask Guide toTake Fast Action in Times of Quarantine and Beyond

Nina Webster

Table of Contents

Introduction

You are worried about catching the coronavirus (COVID-19) and spreading the disease in times when quality equipment to protect against viruses is hard to get by. You want to know the basics about diseases and their spreading and you want actionable steps to make sure you and your loved ones do not catch the virus. COVID-19 has taken the world by storm, and many worry about the best way to protect themselves and keep the virus out.

If you want a solution that is easy to use and can keep you and others safe, then this guidebook is for you. As you read through, you will learn the different life-saving measures that anyone can take to protect themselves and others against infections and viruses. Also, this book will enable and empower you to take the necessary actions immediately through a step-by-step guide of quality medical face masks and virus-proof sanitizing solutions. All of these can be made from the comfort of your own home, providing you protection in any situation.

My name is Nina Webster, and as a critical care doctor in New York, I have experienced the horrific consequences of hospitals being overwhelmed with patients, trying to fight this invisible killer whilst working with a scarcity of resources. It seemed like yesterday when the spreading of COVID-19 was just a rumor in the city, a large cause of the spread was that we did not know how to defend against it. Fortunately, we now have much more knowledge about the prevention of the spreading of the illness to others. In order to prevent other cities from being ravaged by this outbreak, I want to show you that we can fight off this infectious virus with these proven preventative measures.

Once you have read this guidebook, you will have all the power and knowledge to save lives by making your own reusable medical face masks and sanitizing solutions at home, all guaranteed to work well. If you make your own hand sanitizers and sanitizing solutions from home, you are able to make sure that they work well. Homemade solutions will only have the ingredients you add to them, making them safe and more effective than store-bought options any day.

Preventative measures against viruses have proven to be able to stop transmission and dramatically decrease the number of influenza cases. I have seen with my own eyes that if everyone works together, we can put the infection of the disease to a halt. According to the CDC, individuals who want to prevent themselves from getting coronavirus, and prevent the spread of the disease must avoid close contact, wash their hands often, use a hand sanitizer which has a minimum of 60 percent alcohol and wear face masks.

This guidebook will help protect you with two of these aspects. We will look at how to create our own face masks that will filter out dust and germs and can keep you safe when you do need to go out and be around other people. Then we will also look at how to make your own hand sanitizers and disinfectants to make it less likely for the virus to spread around you. When you make these products on your own, you decrease your own risks and make it easier to know what ingredients are in the products you use.

With the help and expertise that this book provides, you will be able to help others save lives by teaching them the importance of hygiene and you will be saving them and you a lot of money because it is not necessary to buy expensive medical equipment anymore.

Learn everything you need to know about making your own DIY homemade medical face mask and sanitizing solutions using materials you already have at home, including important tips for caring for your masks towards the protection against germs, bacteria, and infectious diseases.

This is easier to do than you would think. You may be tempted to go and spend a lot of money on the latest masks or have to be at the mercy of whether the store has the hand sanitizer that you want. With the help of this guidebook, you can make your own and always have the products that you need to stay safe, without having to worry about spreading the disease in the meantime.

The knowledge and guidelines that you are about to read are proven to yield incredible results in the battle against even the deadliest pandemic of your time. Every chapter in this book will empower you more to bust myths about disease spread, personal hygiene, physical contact and will provide you with vital information that will help you stay healthy and prevent the spreading of infectious viruses and bacteria. If you follow the guidelines in this book, it is very likely that you will save the life of a loved one, and you will be assured that you and your family are safe from any and all pandemics.

The COVID-19 pandemic took the world by storm. Many were not prepared and that allowed the virus to spread like crazy in many areas, including New York. Now that we know more about this virus and how it works, we can take the right steps to avoid getting sick and can even protect those around us. This guidebook will show you how to get it done. Take some time to read through this guidebook and learn how to make your own face masks, hand sanitizers, and disinfectants to keep you safe during this pandemic.

Chapter 1:

Most Important Information You Need to Know in Order to Stay Safe

With all the confusion going on concerning COVID-19 and the different news sources telling something new each day, it is hard to know where to start or where we stand when it comes to this virus. Having the facts down does nothing but protect us and ensures that we actually know how to handle the virus along the way. In this chapter, we will explore some of the important information that helps us understand what a virus is, how they can harm humans, and what to expect as COVID continues to spread.

What is a Virus, and What are Bacteria?

There is a lot that is unknown about viruses, but we do know that viruses are quite diverse. Unlike some of the other biological entities, some viruses, including poliovirus, have RNA genomes. Then there are other viruses, like the herpes virus, that have DNA instead. The difference here is that RNA genomes are single-stranded forms of genetic material while DNA possesses two strands that are paired together.

This is just one way that viruses can be different from one another. Their replication strategies and the structures are really diverse as well. So, how do we tell that the biological entity we see is actually a virus and not something else? There are a few features that all viruses, no matter how diverse they are, will share together. First, these viruses are small, coming in with a diameter smaller than 200 nanometers. The second similarity is that they can replicate only inside a host cell. Third, there isn't any virus out there that contains a ribosome, which is a component of the cell's protein-making translational machinery.

A virus is basically a genetic material that is found within an organic particle. It has to invade a host, usually a human, but some viruses can affect other animals in order to survive. These viruses do not have the necessary parts to thrive and grow on their own. They need to use the metabolic processes of their host to help produce a new generation and for them to keep growing and producing.

The way that a virus can accomplish this will vary. Some can insert all of their genetic material into the DNA of the host. Then, it will sit right there and wait until it can translate that information later on. As the cells of the host start to replicate, the virus can do the same thing, creating new virions for spreading. Viruses are also able to burst the cells of the host as they expand in numbers, which is known as a lytic cycle of reproduction.

How large are Viruses?

The word virus actually comes to us from the Latin word meant to describe a liquid that is poisonous. This is because the early forms of finding and imaging the microbes weren't able to capture these tiny particles. The sizes of the virus will vary. The porcine Circovirus is just 17 nanometers wide, and then there are some that are a lot bigger, like the Tupanvirus, with a diameter of 2.3 micrometers. They can come in a wide range of complexities as well. Some have their own unique proteins and are surrounded by an array of envelopes and shells to assist in how they can infect and reproduce just about every species throughout the world. This is why we can find viruses that will be able to infect humans and some that are better suited towards certain animals.

Because viruses vary so much in size, structure, and type, it is hard to know how you can fight against them to prevent them from hijacking your cells and making you sick. It is incredibly easy to catch viruses in general just due to their biological design as infiltrators that will remain inert until the conditions for spreading are just right, and since they all exist in different forms with different modes of transmissions and locations of infections, it is hard to fight them off. No blanket solution is perfect for preventing the transmission of viruses, but there are precautions that you can take and those will make all the difference. You can learn to protect yourself, to prevent as much as you can, but in reality, when you are dealing with something as small as standard virions, there is very little that you can do to keep them all out. However, if you can prevent them from getting to where they need to be in order to infect your body, you can prevent yourself from getting ill. This is why we wash our hands and wear masks—when we block off the standard routes that viruses can use to get to where they infect us, we prevent them from ever being able to spread in the first place.

Types of Viruses Harmful to Humans

Most viruses are not much fun to deal with. The cold or flu viruses, for example, are two types of viruses that we often encounter that can be unpleasant when we get them, but aren't necessarily harmful to people. We are out of work for a few days and have to stay in bed, but everyone knows that as time goes on, and with a little rest, those viruses will be gone and we can go back to life. There are a few viruses that can be a bit more serious to humans, and these are the ones that we need to be especially cautious of. A few examples of viruses that are harmful to humans include:

1. **Polio**: At the height of the pandemic, 13,000 cases involved paralysis and 1000 deaths yearly from this disease. And many of these deaths were children.
2. **Virus Mad Cow**: This was called mad cow disease for a number of years. This is a disease that is transmitted to the victim through meat that was contaminated. There are a number of symptoms, including loss of control over the muscles and the nervous system, and dementia. If left untreated, it leads to death.

3. **Rabies**: This is one that many have heard of, though they may not consider it a virus. It will cause difficulty with swallowing, foaming at the mouth, a fear of water, delusions, and even anger. This is spread through the saliva of animals and often through bites from dogs. It can attach the nervous system and can be lethal when it reaches the brain.
4. **HIV and AIDS:** These are two variations of the same virus. This one will attack the immune system, and for many years, it was a death sentence with no cure if someone got this one.

The good news is that the more we study about viruses and how they work, the more likely that a vaccine can be developed. This makes the likelihood that these viruses, and others that are similar, will be treated and won't be as deadly and harmful to humans in the future.

How Long Does it Take to Make a Vaccine?

There are many viruses that used to have huge impacts on humans, killing thousands a year. And today, thanks to vaccines, many of those same viruses are no longer around and don't pose the threat that they once did. But, how long does it take to make one of these vaccines? And how long do we need to wait for a vaccine to come out for the COVID virus? We will answer that first question here.

In 1902, the U.S. Congress passed an act that would regulate the sale of serums, toxins, viruses, and other analogous products. This was later referred to as the Biologics Control Act. This was one of the first federal legislation put into effect to help control the quality of drugs. This act emerged as a response to the contamination events that happened in St. Louis in 1901 involving the vaccine for smallpox and the antitoxin for diphtheria.

This act then created the Hygienic Laboratory of the U.S. Public Health Service to oversee the manufacture of biological drugs. This then turned into the National Institutes of Health later on. The point of this Act helped to establish that the government had the right to control all the establishments that were making vaccines. Then in the United States Public Service Act of 1944, it was required that the federal government would issue licenses for biological products, and that included vaccines. After there was an accident with the poliovirus vaccine in 1954, the Division of Biologics Standards was then formed to oversee the regulation and safety of vaccines.

The whole point of this was to regulate some of the vaccines that were created and to make sure that the vaccines were as safe and secure for people to take and use as possible. This was a bit of a challenge and sometimes slowed down how quickly the viruses would receive a vaccine because of some of the red tape put up. The point, though, was to prevent some horrible accidents and other issues for patients and make the vaccines safer for everyone.

Thanks to these Acts and government regulation, there are a few different stages that a vaccine needs to go through during development and testing. The first stages are more exploratory in nature. Oversight and regulation will increase as the potential vaccine goes through the process to ensure that it is safe for those who use it. Some of the stages found in making a vaccine include:

1. The exploratory stage

This is all about the research. Depending on the virus and the amount of funding behind it, this stage can take between two to four years. Scientists in academia and from the government will search for and work with natural or synthetic antigens that could help to treat or prevent a specific disease. These could include weakened viruses or bacteria, virus-like particles, or something else that would help prevent the patient from suffering from the disease.

2. Pre-Clinical Stage

These studies would use the cell-culture or the tissue-culture systems and some animal testing to see how safe the potential vaccine is, and whether it actually works at all. Animal subjects will usually include monkeys and mice. These studies will give the researchers a good idea of what kind of response they would get out of humans, though this is not always perfect. They may even figure out a safe starting dose to use later as they do more research and study.

Researchers can sometimes adopt a candidate vaccine during this state to help make it as effective as possible, with as few side effects as possible. They can do some challenge studies with animals. This means that they would use the potential vaccine on the animals, and then try to infect them with the target pathogen to see what will happen.

There are a lot of potential vaccines that never get past this stage. This is because, even with a lot of good ideas, many products will fail to get the right response out of the immune system. There may need to be a few rounds to get past this stage, and it takes one to two years.

3. IND Application

A sponsor, which can often be a private company, will submit an application for Investigational New Drugs through the Food and Drug Administration in the United States. The sponsor will need to describe the manufacturing and the testing processes and summarize the reports of the lab. They need to have steps laid out for how the study will be done. Then a review board will look through the information, and within 30 days, they will approve the application or not.

4. The Vaccine Trials

If the potential vaccine gets through the IND application, it is time to enter the first phase known as vaccine trials. This is going to involve smaller groups of adults to see how the vaccine will work on them. If this particular vaccine is meant for children, this first phase will start with adults, and then they will move down the age until they reach the target instead of starting right in children. Phase one trials can be non-blinded, which means that the researchers and sometimes even the subjects will know whether a placebo or a vaccine is used.

The goal with this one is to assess how safe the potential vaccine is, and then figure out how good the immune response is for this vaccine. Researchers may find, in some cases, that it is time to challenge the model, which means that they will infect the participants with the targeted pathogen and see how it works. If this does happen, the subjects are monitored, and the conditions are controlled.

5. The Vaccine Trial

If the last stage went well and the vaccine continued to show results, then it is time to move on to the vaccine trials. This is when several hundred individuals will try the vaccine and see how successful they are. These trials will be controlled and randomized, and there will be a placebo group. The goal with this is to see how safe the vaccine is, whether it does what they say and if they can find a good schedule to recommend the vaccine to others.

6. Phase 3 Vaccine Trials

Potential vaccines that make it through the last stage will move into some really big trails that can involve thousands, and sometimes tens of thousands, of people in them. These are randomized and even double-blind. They will often include the experimental vaccine and a placebo to see what the effects are in both. The goal of this one is to see how safe the vaccine is for a lot of people at once. It is possible that with the smaller groups, there are rare side effects that won't show up, so these larger studies allow us to see whether that is true or not.

The effectiveness of the vaccine is tested during this as well. This testing includes whether the vaccine actually prevents the disease. Does it help to prevent infection with the pathogen? And does it lead to the production of antibodies or some other types of responses in the immune system related to that pathogen? The answer is, hopefully, yes.

7. Approval and Licensure

Once the vaccine has done well through all the other steps, it is time to go through and get it approved and license it. The developer needs to submit a Biologics License Application to the FDA. The FDA will look over all the details and the work that is done and can then approve the labeling of the vaccine.

Even after this, the FDA will continue to monitor the production of the vaccine to make sure that the company maintains the proper procedures, and the vaccine continues to be safe. In the meantime, the company can continue to make the vaccine and often will start to distribute it out. This vaccine will hopefully save a lot of lives and keep people from getting sick. Sometimes additional studies will be done to make sure that the vaccine continues to be safe, and they may check whether there are other potential uses for it.

How Long Will the COVID-19 Vaccine Take to Make?

There has been a lot of talk about whether a vaccine for the current COVID-19 pandemic will come out soon. After looking at the timeline that we discussed above, we may find that this is a process that could take a number of years. In fact, most vaccines take a minimum of five years to develop, if not much longer, if the first vaccine that is tried is not effective.

With the vaccine potentially taking that long, many people worry that it will be too late. There is a little hope that this process can be sped up because of the interest in the vaccine, and the possibility that several research companies may come together to make it happen faster. But do we really want a vaccine that was sped along? The other process may take a bit longer to work with, but this is done to make sure that the vaccine is effective and safe. It can be infuriating, but it is for the safety of those who rely on it.

With this in mind, it is better to find other methods to prevent the spread of COVID-19. It is likely that by the time the vaccine comes out, it will be too late, and most people will already develop immunity on their own. Protecting ourselves using the guidelines that we will talk about in the next chapter and creating our own disinfectants, masks, and hand sanitizers, as we will discuss later on, maybe the best course of action compared to waiting for a vaccine.

Safety Guidelines

Knowing the most common safety guidelines is critical to making sure that we can stay safe and protect others. Several prominent organizations make it their job to provide guidelines that work. We will explore the WHO (World Health

Organization), and the CDC to help us understand our roles in staying safe from this pandemic.

WHO Guidelines

The World Health Organization has provided a number of safety guidelines that are meant to keep us safe during the pandemic. These include:

1. Thoroughly and regularly clean your hands. Do a combination of washing them with water and soap or using an alcohol-based hand rub. Washing our hands with soap and water or with a hand sanitizer can make sure that any virus on our hands is killed.
2. Maintain at least three feet between people. When someone speaks, sneezes, and coughs, they can spray small liquid droplets. These may contain the virus if the person is infected. If two or more people stay too close to one another, it is possible to breathe in these droplets and get sick.
3. Avoid places with lots of people. When more people come together in one place, it is more likely that you will be in contact with someone infected (sometimes without knowing) with COVID-19. It is

also harder to maintain the right distance in a large group.

4. Do not touch your mouth, nose, or eyes. Your hand touches many surfaces during the day. One of these may have the COVID virus on them and can easily spread to you.
5. Follow good respiratory hygiene. This means using a bent elbow or even a tissue when you sneeze or cough rather than your hand. Wash your hands right after.
6. If you experience symptoms like milk fever, headache, or a cough, stay home and self-isolate until those symptoms are gone. Try to get someone else to bring you supplies. If you must leave the house, then wear a mask to avoid infecting others.
7. If you have difficulty breathing, a cough, and a fever, seek medical attention. It is best to call ahead to see what instructions the medical facility has in place.
8. Keep up to date on all the latest information, but make sure to use trusted sources. The WHO and national and local health authorities are a good source to use. Local and national authorities will help advise you on the right steps to take to protect yourself.

CDC Guidelines

It doesn't take long looking at the guidelines to see that the CDC and the WHO have very similar guidelines that can be useful for keeping us safe and protected against the virus. Some of the rules with the CDC are more specific and can help answer questions people may have along the way. Some of the CDC guidelines include:

1. Know how the virus spreads. Studies show that the virus can be spread from one person to the next and those who are close to one another (usually within six feet). It can be spread through respiratory droplets and even from those who do not show symptoms.
2. Wash your hands: Do this often. Use soap and water for 20 seconds, especially after sneezing, coughing, blowing your nose, or being in a public place.
    a. If there is no soap and water around, use a hand sanitizer. This must have a minimum of 60 percent alcohol. Make sure to cover all the surfaces of the hand and then rub until the hands feel dry.
    b. Do not touch the mouth, nose, or eyes with hands that are not washed.

3. Avoid close contact: Avoid being close to others who are sick, even if you are in your own home. If it is possible, maintain six feet between the one who is sick and everyone else in your home. There should also be some distance between yourself and others who are not at home. Some rules to follow include:
    a. It is possible that those without symptoms can spread the virus.
    b. Stay six feet or more away from other people.
    c. Do not go together with others into a big group.
4. Cover mouth and nose with a cloth face cover when you go out. It is possible to spread this virus when you don't show any symptoms. It is a good idea to wear a covering when you need to go out in public.
    a. Do not place these on children younger than two, and do not add to someone who already struggles with breathing.
    b. These face coverings will protect others to make sure that they don't get sick.

    c. Do not take a facemask that is meant for a worker in the healthcare field.
    d. Even with the mask, it is important to practice the social distancing above.
5. Cover sneezes and coughs: If you are inside a private setting and do not have a mask on, always cover the nose and mouth when you sneeze or cough. A tissue or the inside of the elbow is best. Wash your hands when you are done using the rules above.
6. Clean and disinfect: These need to be done on surfaces that are touched on a daily basis, including faucets, sinks, keyboards, handles, counters, light switches, doorknobs, and more.
    a. If a surface is dirty, then it is time to clean it. Use detergent or some soap to help.
    b. Then use a household disinfectant or make one of your own.
7. Monitor health. Always be alert to any symptoms that you have. Take your temperature to see whether there are any issues. There is a variety of CDC guidance to follow if you develop symptoms. `

These guidelines are important to follow to make sure that you, and those around you, can stay safe during the pandemic. If we are able to follow the simple guidelines above, it is possible to slow down the spread of this infection, even without a vaccine.

Chapter 2:

Why Hand Sanitizers and Medical Face Masks Are Absolutely Vital

One aspect that both the WHO and the CDC recommend for preventing the spread of COVID-19 is to wear masks and to use hand sanitizers, especially if there is no soap and water nearby. These are the two most important things that you can do when it is necessary to go out in public, which most of us have to do at one point or another. These actions seem simple, but they are enough to keep us and others safe. Understanding why they are so important, and what role they can play in the process will be important to see the spread of this virus go down.

What are Hand Sanitizers and Why Do You Need Them?

During this pandemic, many people feel confused due all the information that is handed out. We hear the words disinfectant, sanitizer, and cleaner, and it is hard to differentiate between them. To make it even harder, there are products that will combine two of these words together. With all this confusion, what are the differences between these three categories?

To keep it simple, sanitizers will reduce the bacteria that is on any surface by at least 99.9%. The disinfectant, on the other hand, will kill a wider range of microorganisms. And then cleaners are just there to remove soils, dirt, and other impurities from the surface, but they don't really sanitize or kill off the different bacteria.

That is a simple idea of how this works, but there is a little bit more to it. To start, disinfectants and sanitizers are regulated thanks to the EPA, and that means that they need to meet certification. These products must go through various tests and meet certain criteria before they can put those words on the label. By law, it is illegal to label a product as a disinfectant or a sanitizer until the EPA has certified it as such. That helps us to know that we can actually trust the efficacy of the product.

Both disinfectants and sanitizers have to be tested against certain germs. Chemical labels have to list out which germs are specifically and individually. This is why we can have one disinfectant that is able to kill germs A and B, but then another one that is responsible for killing germs B and C. It is important to remember that while these products are great to use, there isn't a single product on the market that can kill all microorganisms. You need to know which germs the product you use will protect against, and only choose products that will kill and eliminate the germs you do not want. Sanitizers will work just for bacteria, while disinfectants may help kill fungi, mildew, mold, and viruses.

The time that it takes to kill germs and bacteria will be important when evaluating the disinfectants and sanitizers, and this is something the company must list on their label. Some chemicals can take up to five minutes, and others will take less than a minute. This will be known as the dwell time, and you should consider them before purchasing or using any of these products.

One thing to note about sanitizers is that they are often used in settings for food service, but not always. If a product is labeled as a sanitizer for food contact, then it is one that we can safely use on surfaces that will touch food. Follow the instructions for using these then give it time to dry before you start putting food on the surface.

A good way to remember the differences between the disinfectants, sanitizers, and cleaners include the following:

1. Sanitizers are there to kill certain types of bacteria in a specific time period, and the EPA will regulate them.
2. Disinfectants will kill more microorganisms, including fungi, mildews, viruses, and bacteria, during a specific period of time. These also have some EPA regulations.
3. Cleaners are useful for removing dirt, but they are not responsible for getting rid of microorganisms like the other options.

How Can They Protect Against Illness?

Now that we know a little more about hand sanitizers and how they vary from all the different types of disinfectants and cleaners out there, we need to learn how they can protect us against illness. And the first place to look at is what is inside the hand sanitizer we use.

The answer to this will vary based on what brand we use. However, most options will contain alcohol that is suspended in a gel. The alcohol is the part that will kill the germs, and then the gel

is responsible for soothing the hands. It also helps prevent rapid evaporation of the alcohol in the first place.
The alcohol that is used is either isopropyl alcohol or ethyl alcohol, though some products will use a combination of both. Ethyl alcohol is drinking alcohol, and it is the exact same kind found in alcoholic beverages. Isopropyl alcohol is the same kind that we find in rubbing alcohol. They are similar chemicals and can work the same way in preventing the spread of illness.

Note here that there are some hand sanitizers that do not have alcohol in them at all. They will use a different cleaning agent that can be effective against certain types of bacteria. These are not effective against COVID-19, and they don't prevent against certain types of flu and other viruses, so they are not a good choice to go with. COVID-19 and other similar viruses are best prevented when the hand sanitizer solution has a minimum of 60 percent alcohol, so those are the kinds that are best to use.

With that in mind, we need to look at what hand sanitizers are all about and how they can protect us. These sanitizers are not effective against a few different types of viruses, which is why we have disinfectants. Those viruses that do not have an external membrane can not be prevented with these hand sanitizers. However, COVID-19 viruses do have this membrane, and so we can use these sanitizers to fight off and protect against them.

There are two ways that hand sanitizers can protect against coronavirus. First, it will disrupt the external membrane so that the virus is killed. The second way these can protect is that they strip the oil from the skin, the same oil that tends to harbor the virus and other bacteria as well. This makes it harder for bacteria and viruses to get on your hand and stick while killing any that may have found their way onto the skin.

Hand sanitizers will only work, though if you use them right. It is important to cover your hands completely with the sanitizer, both front and back, and then rub vigorously until they dry completely. This will take twenty seconds or so, which is about the same amount of time as washing our hands properly.

Different Types of Sanitizing Solutions

There are a few different types of sanitizing solutions we can use based on our goals and what we like the best. Finding a good brand that will provide us with the protection we want will be critical as we go through the pandemic and after as well. The main types of sanitizing solutions we can use include:

Soap: These are the kinds we can use while washing our hands. They provide an added layer of protection because we can wash our hands, clean them off, and still get the same protection and disinfecting that we would with other solutions. Make sure that the soap you choose has the power to fight off the particular viruses that you want, and then use the solution any time that you wash your hands.

Gel: The option most people think about when they hear hand sanitizer is gel. Often these are capable of going with us, and they are used any time we touch a surface that may be dirty, or we want to keep clean throughout the day but can't make it to a sink all the time.

Hand wipes: Hand wipes can be used along with the other two options, though they are usually reserved for wiping down other surfaces, like doorknobs and cart handles.

Other Uses of Hand Sanitizers

Hand sanitizer is a great way to keep us safe and make sure that viruses can't infect us. There are a few other neat uses for a hand sanitizer that we can use along the way as well, and knowing what these are can be a lot of fun. Some of the other ways that we can use hand sanitizer include:

1. Disinfect other items: This can be used to keep other items and areas of high traffic safe. This would include keyboard and mouse for your computer. Use it to clean the handle of a grocery cart, your doorknobs, and more to keep the germs out.
2. Shine a cell phone screen: Add a tiny bit onto a phone screen, not enough to soak it, and rub with a cloth. This will get rid of the oil and smudges and can help disinfect from all the other things you touch before touching the screen.
3. Removes stains: When you have a big stain to use, a bit of hand sanitizer can blot out all the stains. This works well on clothing and whiteboards and almost any other surface. Test it on a smaller part to make sure there isn't damage to the surface first.
4. A treatment for acne: Adding a little bit to a bump of acne on your face with a cotton swab can help. The alcohol that is inside the solution will dry the acne out and can reduce the redness and itching.

5. Glue remover: If there is some sticky residue from price tags or labels or other places where the glue just won't leave, then a bit of hand sanitizer on that adhesive will be enough to take care of the problem.
6. Hair gel: With a little bit of sanitizer, you can help get your hair nice and smooth. Do this while the hair is wet. Scented hand sanitizers work well for this, so you don't get the bad smells as you go along.
7. Sunglass or eyeglass cleaner: This works just as well as some of the special cleaners and can be a lot easier to work with as well.
8. Cleaning questionable areas: Hand sanitizer can help clean up other areas when you are in public, including public toilets and other places that you don't want to touch. Add a bit to the area and scrub, and you are safe again.

Why are Face Masks Important?

In addition to using hand sanitizer to prevent the virus from getting to your system, using a face mask can be useful as well. A face mask is a barrier device used to control infections to prevent health care providers from coughing or breathing on patients. It is also used to prevent sneezes and spit from making contact with the eyes or face of anyone. It is meant to cover the mouth and nose of the person who is trying to prevent the spread of disease and viruses.

Wearing a face mask is meant to prevent the spread of infections, and it will help prevent an individual from contracting infectious germs through the air. When someone sneezes, coughs, or talks, it is possible they will release germs into the air, and these germs can infect those who are near. Face masks are part of an infection control strategy meant to eliminate cross-contamination.

So basically, they can help prevent you from getting sick by preventing the particles from getting off someone else, or from the air, to your system through your normal breathing. They can also protect others because the mask will prevent you from spreading germs to other people, keeping those germs trapped and safe inside the mask.

Why Do Doctors Recommend Face Masks?

The CDC recommends the wearing of cloth face coverings or masks in public settings that could make it hard to practice the etiquette of social distancing. But is there any science behind wearing these masks? There are several doctors who believe that these face masks can be the protection that many people need when going out in public. According to Dr. Aaron Hamilton, MD, "Wearing a cloth face mask is recommended as an extra layer of protection. That means that you should still be following any shelter in place orders in your community. But when you are venturing out to the grocery store, pharmacy, or hospital, it's wise to wear one."

Do They Work?

Many people question whether these masks work or not for their intended purpose. CDC experts say that several recent studies show that a large portion of individuals who have coronavirus don't display any symptoms. This means the individuals are asymptomatic. To make it even worse, those who do develop symptoms can spread the virus to others long before any of the symptoms show up. This means that individuals with the virus, whether they show symptoms at some point or not, can spread it to a lot of other people along the way.

It is possible for this virus to spread between those who stand less than six feet apart, whether they sneeze, cough, or simply talk to one another. This will hold true whether none of these individuals notice the common symptoms of COVID-19 or not. The masks may be the solution that we need to make sure that, even when we don't show symptoms, we can stay protected.

According to Dr. Hamilton, and other professionals in the field, a cloth mask is not going to prevent you from breathing in some of the droplets that can carry a virus, whether it is COVID-19 or another virus. But it can help protect others from you if you are the one infected, whether you display symptoms or not. These cloth masks help to reinforce social distancing, which can help to slow down how much the virus spreads.

Who Needs to Wear a Mask?

Masks can be helpful for most people when it is time to stop the spread of viruses. There are a few people who should never put on a face mask according to guidance from the CDC:

1. Children who are under the age of 2.
2. Anyone who has some breathing difficulties.
3. Anyone who is incapacitated, unconscious, or who is not able to take the face mask off without some help.

How to Wear the Face Covering

There are also a few rules that come to us from the CDC when it is time to make sure the face covering is put on well and will keep us safe. Some of the rules to keep in mind any time we wear a face covering or a mask include:

1. It should be nice and snug, while maintaining comfort, against the sides of your face.
2. You need to secure it with ear loops or ties.
3. It should have more than one layer of material.
4. It should still allow us to breathe without restrictions, so we don't cause more problems from that.
5. It should be one that we can wear and then wash through the machine. When it goes through machine washing and drying, the material should not change shape or get damaged.

How Do Masks Protect Us?

The masks can help protect us in more than one way. First, they will prevent you from getting sick. COVID-19, and other viruses, can stay in the air around us. When others breathe, cough, or even talk, particles can end up in the air. Sometimes these include particles of viruses, including COVID-19, without the individual showing signs or symptoms they are sick. Then when you walk by, you can breathe in those same particles without even noticing. Without a mask, it is hard to filter those particles through, and you can end up sick and dealing with multiple symptoms just for walking about without being around those who are sick themselves.

Wearing a mask can help protect you. When you walk around, the masks will help filter out the particles and will make sure they don't end up in your own system. This keeps you safe and sound and can keep coronavirus and other similar viruses out of your system.

Another reason to wear a mask is to protect others. Many individuals can be carriers of COVID-19 without noticing any symptoms at all. It is possible to be a carrier and not show any signs or symptoms even if you are an otherwise healthy individual. This means that your coughs and sneezes and talking could release particles of the virus, without you realizing that others may get sick.

Wearing a mask in this situation will help to protect others. Again, you will trap the particles of coronavirus and other viruses inside the mask, and make it difficult for others to catch them.

Wearing a mask not only protects yourself, but it protects those around you.

Masks and hand sanitizers are simple measures that we can use to keep safe from all the viruses of the world, not just coronavirus. Knowing how to use them properly, and how well they can work at keeping us safe will make sure that we stop the spread of this disease in no time.

Chapter 3:

Personal Hygiene – How to Make Yourself and Others Virus-Proof

The first line of defense against any virus is your own personal hygiene. Having the right tools to know how to wash your hands and keep them safe will make life so much easier. We can't avoid coming into contact with every virus, but washing our hands and using medical face masks can make life a lot easier and can keep us protected.

Washing Your Hands

The first rule of staying healthy is to wash your hands. Doing this on a regular basis is a simple yet effective way to make sure that you aren't spreading germs that can hurt you and those around you. Knowing how to wash your hands, the health benefits of washing your hands, and even when to wash your hands can all be important to get this right. Washing your hands can help to prevent the spread of many diseases.

The Health Benefits of Washing Your Hands

There are many benefits to washing your hands on a regular basis. In addition to preventing the spread of COVID-19 and other diseases, hand washing can help us to stay safe and healthy. The first benefit is that hand washing will help to prevent intestinal problems. Many types of viruses are spread through the skin and from not taking care of our surroundings or keeping our hands washed.

In fact, proper handwashing is seen as the best way to protect yourself and others from being exposed to COVID-19 and other harmful viruses. To combat COVID-19, the CDC recommends that individuals regularly wash their hands with water and soap for a minimum of 20 seconds, especially when they have blown their nose, coughed, sneezed, or have been in a public area.

Washing our hands properly, using running water and soap, can keep illnesses away, whether you have a healthy immune system or you are dealing with a weakened immune system. Handwashing can help protect you from not only COVID-19 but also from other respiratory infections, such as pneumonia. In addition, it can also help to prevent the spread of gastric or other types of infections as well. Many of these conditions can even potentially be fatal for vulnerable populations, such as the elderly, the immunocompromised, and the very young. It is possible to pass on these terms, even when you are not sick, and handwashing can slow down the spread with relatively little work.

When Should You Wash Your Hands?

While you don't need to spend all day in the bathroom washing your hands, there are a few important rules about hand washing that we need to keep in mind along the way. It is pretty obvious to most people that they need to wash their hands regularly, but how often is up to debate from one person to another. And many wonder if it is possible to wash your hands too much.

There isn't a daily quota of hand washing that you need to follow to keep healthy. It often depends on the environment you are in and what you accomplish during the day. If you are around a lot of other people or doing work or going to the store, then you may need to wash your hands more often than you would just be staying at home for the day. A few of the general rules that everyone can follow when it comes to washing your hands include:

1. After you use the bathroom.
2. Before you eat or even touch your food.
3. Any time that your hands get dirty.
4. After you are using objects that are known for harboring viruses and bacteria, this can include doorknobs, steering wheels, phones, grocery carts, and more.
5. Wash after you cough or sneeze into your hands.

It is easier for children who are closely monitored to keep their hands cleaned if they are reminded to. On the other hand, it is more likely that adults will get caught up with their daily activities, and that makes them more likely to overlook healthy hand washing. Knowing the positive impact of handwashing on your life and your family, and reminding yourself of why it is so important will make it easier to stick with the goals here.

How to Wash Your Hands

It never hurts to review hand washing and how to get this done to keep ourselves safe. According to the Harvard Medical School health publications, it is important to run your hands together for a minimum of 15 seconds after applying soap. When this is done, it is time to rinse your hands under some warm tap water to remove the soap.

A good hand washing will require us to focus on the back of the hands, the palms, and the fingertips to get everything taken care of. Some of the other steps we must remember when washing our hands to make sure all the germs are gone include:

1. Turn on the water and get it warm. Get your hands wet by placing them under the tap for a few seconds.
2. Rub the soap all over the palms as well as the back of the hands. Cover every area of your hands.
3. When there is enough lather created, keep rubbing your palms together.
4. Rub the palm of one of your hands over the back of your second hand. You can run the fingers through each other at the same time. Repeat for both hands.
5. Rub your palms together at this point, making sure to run your fingers through one another as well.
6. With your fingers of one hand, you can run the back of your finger on the other hand and then repeat this with your other hand.
7. Rub your thumbs into the palm of each hand using circular motions.

8. Take your fingers of one hand in the palm of the other and then rub again in a circular motion, repeating with both hands.
9. When this is done, you can rinse both hands with water.
10. Dry your hands with a paper towel if possible, and then use that towel to turn the tap off, so you don't get the germs back onto the handle.

This process should take about twenty seconds to complete. Sing a short song, like the ABC's to help you keep track of how much time has passed or you can set a timer when you get started. This is the amount of time it takes to wash the hands thoroughly and will make it easier to keep those germs away.

How and When to Use Hand Sanitizer

Hand sanitizer can be an important part of our routine as well. This helps to keep our hands clean from different surfaces, especially when we can't be near soap and water to wash our hands. But we need to make sure we are using the hand sanitizer correctly, or it won't perform the way that we want.

In Your House

In your home, there are several times when you would need to use hand sanitizer. After sneezing or coughing, it is recommended that you use hand sanitizer to keep your hands free of germs. You can also use this any time that you are working with food, touching surfaces that may have germs, and more.

Using hand sanitizer at home is usually not as prevalent, though, as in public areas. The areas of our homes are often cleaner than in public areas. And when we sneeze or cough or go to the bathroom, it is often easier to just wash our hands instead of using hand sanitizer all the time. It is still possible to use it, and keeping some around is never a bad thing when dealing with the protection against germs.

In Public

It is more common that hand sanitizer is used when we are in public areas. There are more chances for germs in public places because more people are present, and not all of them follow proper hygiene and handwashing protocols. It is a good idea to bring some hand sanitizer around with you in public because many opportunities will present themselves, but it isn't always possible to get near a sink to wash your hands.

Some areas where it is best to use hand sanitizer will include:

1. Restrooms. It is best to wash your hands after using a restroom, but it may be a good idea to bring in the sanitizer as well. According to a 2106 Bradley Corp. survey of 1000 respondents, 67 percent admitted that they skipped the soap and just used water after using a public restroom. And 82 percent said they skipped handwashing as well. This makes it really important to have a backup option near the doors and sinks to make sure that germs can't leave the bathroom with you.
2. Exits and entrances: It is possible for a single doorknob to have a lot of germs on it. According to a report by CBS, within two to four hours, a virus that was placed onto a doorknob was then picked up by up to 60 percent of visitors and workers in the company. In addition to cleaning and disinfecting surfaces that are touched often, make sure to have some hand sanitizing solution after you touch these places.
3. Break rooms, food courts, or cafeterias: There are lots of high traffic touch areas that we need to worry about here. Washing

your hands can help to eliminate the germs, and using some hand sanitizer can help in between.

4. Carts and baskets: If you go to the store and touch a cart or a basket, it is likely that you will end up with some germs. Many other people have touched those areas and may have touched their hair, mouths, noses, and more while touching the carts and handles of baskets as well. Disinfecting these with hand wipes and using hand sanitizer before and after using the cart can make a difference.
5. Transaction counters. In one study that was published by PLOS ONE, researchers swabbed some $1 bills from the bank and then found that there were hundreds of species of microorganisms living on these bills. Other research shows us that pathogens, including E. coli and salmonella, can be found on paper money, and these can lead to some serious illnesses along the way. Bringing some hand sanitizer along when being in these areas can help.

It never hurts to use hand sanitizer on a regular basis. This will make it easier to keep your hands clean when you sneeze or cough, or when you are in another area where germs are highly prevalent. It is best to wash your hands, but using these when hand washing is a bit tougher can be effective as well.

Myths About Hand Sanitizers

Ever since hand sanitizers came out, there are a lot of different myths out there about how they work and how effective they can be for keeping you safe. Knowing what the truth is and what the myth is can make it easier to use hand sanitizers the right way. Some of the most common myths include:

1. Hand sanitizers kill 99.9 percent of germs: This claim refers to the lab tests that are done. When we use them in the real world, it is usually closer to 60 percent. This is still quite a bit but shows that it is important to use other precautions as well.
2. All brands of hand sanitizers are the same: If the hand sanitizer isn't at least 60 percent alcohol, it is not going to be effective at reducing how much bacteria are on your hands. There are also different types of alcohol that can be used in these products, and we must be aware of that.
3. Using too much starts to make it ineffective: There are some people who

assume that using too much of the hand sanitizer will make a drug-resistant super bacteria. If you use a sanitizer that mainly made of alcohol, then the germs will be destroyed in contact. This doesn't give the germs a chance to mutate. There have even been studies that show how alcohol-based sanitizers could kill pathogens that were resistant to other drugs and medications.

4. You only need a small amount: You don't need to drown your hands in this, but for the hand sanitizer to be effective, you need to put on enough to rub together the hands for a full twenty seconds before they dry completely.
5. These products can prevent the flu: If you already have the flu virus on your hands, and then use the hand sanitizer, then you may be able to kill off the virus and not be affected. You can still breathe in the flu virus though, so using these products may be able to limit your exposure, but won't guarantee that you are all good.
6. You can use too much hand sanitizer: We have already talked about a few ways this is false. You need enough to make sure you can cover your hands and rub for twenty seconds, and you can't use so much to

make the bacteria resistant to it. If you use it and your hands get dry, go ahead and start using some lotion to help.

How to Use and When to Wear Medical Face Masks

Many organizations recommend wearing face masks. Learning how to use them properly, and when to put them on, can be critical to keeping yourself and others safe. We need to learn how to use and when to wear these face masks to keep everyone safe.

In Your Home and in Public

Healthy adults do not need to wear masks inside their own homes. Disinfecting your home, washing your hands, and using hand sanitizer will be enough to keep you and your family safe. If you are taking care of an individual who is sick, or you have an elderly relative come to visit, then it may be time to wear a mask inside. But for the most part, it is not recommended or required to wear one of these masks in your home.

Some states have required the use of masks for any individual going out in public, and others encourage it without it being a requirement. Knowing how to wear these masks and when they are necessary is important for them to be effective. State health officials advise that everyone, even those who are not sick, wear their face masks when they will leave their home and when they are within six feet of other people. This would include going to the store or another enclosed place.

Those who are sick should stay home. If they do need to go out, they definitely should wear a mask to keep others from getting sick. Everyone else who goes out should wear a mask to prevent the spread of the virus, which they may carry even if they are not sick. Consider wearing a face mask when you are sick with a sneezing or cough illness, or when you expect to be around many other people. The face mask will help protect others from getting your illness.

There are a few guidelines for putting face mask on and taking it off. Some of the guidelines for putting on a face mask when you are going out in public include:

1. Wash your hands with hand sanitizer or soap and water before you touch the mask.
2. Take the mask out of the box and check to see whether there are any tears or other issues on the mask.
3. Determine which part of the mask is considered the top. The side of the mask

that has the stiff bendable edge will be the top and should mold to your nose.

4. Figure out where the top of the mask is located. The colored side, if there is one, is the front and needs to face away from you. The white side should touch your face.
5. Then there are a few instructions to follow based on what mask type you use:
    a. A mask with ear loops: Hole the mask by these loops. Place one of the loops around the ear.
    b. Mask with ties: Bring this to the level of your nose and then place the ties around the head, securing the bow.
    c. Mask with bands: Hold the mask in your hand with the part for the nose on the top of the mask. Allow the headbands to hand below the hands. Bring this to the level of your nose and pull one strap over your head so that it is on the crown. Pull the bottom over your head to let it rest at the nape.
6. Mold the stiff edges to be the shape of your nose.
7. If you have a mask with ties, take the bottom tie, and secure it in place.

8. Pull the bottom of the mask so that it also covers the chin and the mouth.

When you are done using the mask, there are a few steps that you can take to make sure it is safe. Some of the steps for removing your face mask include:

1. Wash your hands with some soap and water before you touch the mask. Avoid touching the front because this is where the contamination will happen. Try to only touch the ties, bands, or loops. Follow the instructions based on the type of mask you have.
    a. Mask with loops: Hold onto both of the loops near the ear and gently lift them to remove the mask.
    b. Mask with ties: Untie the bottom bow and then untie the top part. Pull the mask away as you loosen the ties.
    c. Mask with bands: lift the bottom strap to go over the head and then pull the top strap too.
2. Throw the mask into the trash. Make sure to clean your hands with some hand sanitizer or some soap and water to finish.

How Often Do I Need to Wash?

If you go with a disposable mask, you can simply throw one away when you get home and grab another when it is time to go back out. But many people decide to get their own cloth masks to make things easier and to save money. This is a great idea, but these masks do need to be cleaned regularly to avoid contamination. Most cloth masks can be cleaned in the washer and dryer with your regular clothing, so this can make it easier, but how often should they be cleaned?

There aren't really any hard rules about how often these masks should be cleaned. It will depend on how often you wear the mask. If you would like to be cautious, or you think you were around someone with symptoms, or you coughed or sneezed while using the mask, you can wash it after every use. Having a few different types of masks on hand so you can switch them out each time you want to go in public can help you err on the side of caution without having the washing machine running continuously.

Who Can Wear the Face Masks?

Most people can wear these face masks. There are a few people who should not have them on, but for the most part, healthy adults and most children will be fine wearing masks on a temporary basis when going to the store or being outside. This can help to keep many people safe, so it is a good idea to invest in a few face masks that everyone in the family can use.

There are a few exceptions to this rule, and it is important to know who fits into these categories. First, children under the age of two should not wear these masks. Not only will they struggle with wearing them, but the material and the filtering system could be unsafe for the younger children and can cause more harm than good.

Individuals who have difficulty breathing, including asthma and other similar disorders, may find that wearing a mask can be difficult as well. If these situations pertain to you, then it is best to avoid the masks as well or limit how often they are worn and how often you go out.

If there is an individual who is not able to put the mask on and off themselves or they are incapacitated, then they should not wear a mask, and one should not be put on them. Anytime that the mask would cause more difficulty breathing for the individual, it is better to keep the mask off and not use it at all.

Chapter 4:

Disinfectants – The Most Useful Hand Sanitizers You Need to Have

There is a lot of confusion and misconceptions around hand sanitizers and how they work. Many people assume that all hand sanitizers work the same and that they will kill any and all microorganisms that come around. As we have already discussed, this is not the case, and thinking this way can prove a bad idea. This chapter will take a look at some of the most useful hand sanitizers you need to consider and looks at some of the information that everyone needs to know about using hand sanitizers.

Why Purchase Hand Sanitizers

When fighting off viruses and other pathogens, hand sanitizers can be a great option. While they should not be used as a substitute for handwashing completely, they can add in an extra level of protection when we can't wash our hands or when we want to be extra safe while out in public. If soap and water are not available, it is recommended by the CDC to use a hand sanitizer that is alcohol-based that has at least 60 percent alcohol with it.

Many studies have been done that find that sanitizers with an alcohol concentration between 60 to 95 percent are more effective at killing germs compared to those that have no alcohol in them, or have a lower concentration of alcohol. Hand sanitizers that do not have this high concentration of alcohol may not work well for many of the germs you want to fight off, and some may only reduce the growth of these germs, compared to killing them outright.

While nothing can replace regular handwashing with soap and water, hand sanitizers are a good addition to your routine, especially when dealing with viruses like COVID-19. We can't always make it to the bathroom to wash our hands, and protecting ourselves and others with these hand sanitizers may be the best option to keep us safe and kill off these harmful germs.

Differentiating between Alcoholic and Non-alcoholic Sanitizers

Now we need to take a look at the differences and similarities between two main types of sanitizers out there. The type that the CDC will often recommend is the alcoholic version because it id considered the most effective for killing germs on contact. There are also several non-alcoholic sanitizers out there that are considered good as well, and many claim to be even better than the alcoholic versions. The CDC still claims that the alcohol-based hand sanitizers are the best to use, so we need to understand why this would be, and how the non-alcoholic versions are a bit different.

Most hand sanitizers can be classified as either alcohol-based or alcohol-free. Many people prefer to do the alcohol-based hand sanitizer because they are more efficient, and they are the type that often gets recommended. Let's dive into some of the differences between each of these types of and sanitizers.

Alcohol-based Hand Sanitizers

Alcohol-based hand sanitizers need to have 60 percent alcohol content or above. This helps the solution to kill 99.9 percent of germs on the hand. The higher the percentage of alcohol in the solution, the more germs can be killed when using it. There are a few versions of these solutions that are higher in alcohol content, and these are more effective. Some are lower, and these will not provide the same protection as those with higher concentrations. In fact, it is believed that if the alcohol concentration gets below 60 percent, the solution becomes as effective as non-alcoholic solutions.

It is easy to take hand sanitization with you. Some pocket-sized versions are reliable, have the right concentration of alcohol content in them, and can be carried everywhere. This makes it easier to take along for traveling. And because the FDA shows that these hand sanitizers can reduce the flue and fight off other infections and viruses, including COVID-19, it is a good idea to keep some on hand all the time.

In addition to relying on the alcohol content, these sanitizers will work with friction. As you rub it onto your palms, there is a warmness that is generated from friction. This helps to evaporate the alcohol and the other particles, including germs, making it more efficient overall. No matter how high the alcohol content of these sanitizers is, you need to make sure to use them as directed. If not, they will not be effective. To use these, take a drop of the sanitizer, about the size of a coin, and put it into your palm spread it all over your hand, both front and back. Rub your palm together until the solution is gone, and your hand is dry again. If your hands are a little dry from using it, this is a good sign that the alcohol is killing the germs.

One major complaint of using these systems is that the sanitizer can cause a bit of dryness to your skin when it is used often. If this happens, you may want to switch to a sanitizer that has moisturizers in it. This can be a bit safer on your hands. Look for some that have vitamin E in them to keep the skin saturated and can keep the dryness away as well.

The alcohol-based hand sanitizers are often seen as the most efficient when preventing the spread of illness because they can kill germs on contact. The alcohol content has to be at least 60 percent or it is not high enough to make a real difference. There are a few solutions out there available that allow you to keep your hands moisturized during times when you plan to use these sanitizers often.

Alcohol-Free Sanitizers

Another option that we can choose is alcohol-free sanitizers. Some people like this version because it doesn't dry out your hands as much as the other option, though there is some question on whether it is effective enough to use to prevent the spread of disease It is a great idea, but it is not always a good choice to go with to stay healthy.

There are many researchers and healthcare centers that believe that alcohol-free hand sanitizers are not able to kill off all the viruses, bacteria, and germs like their alcohol-based counterparts can. If this works depends on the brand and how the hand sanitizer is used, but the fact that there is a question on how effective it is can make it a bad choice during the COVID-19 pandemic and for keeping us safe from other viruses that show up.

Many of the hand sanitizers that fit under this category are going to contain quaternary ammonium compounds instead of the alcohol. These agents work a little bit, but they are not nearly as effective as using alcohol. This makes them less than ideal to use in the first place.

Some people choose to go with these for a variety of reasons. First, they do not dry out the hands as much as the alcohol-based versions. They create little foam afterward and can keep the hands moisturized. For those with already dry skin, they can be preferable. They also do not have any fragrance because most of these sanitizers will be water-based foam. Most of these will contain mainly water and some vitamin E to help moisturize the hands. For those who have dry hands or sensitive hands, these are good, but often they are not effective, and no major health organization really recommends these, so they are not the best choice to go with.

The Best Hand Sanitizers Based on your Situation

There are a lot of situations we encounter each day, and each one will bring in new opportunities to be around germs. And we already discussed how each hand sanitizer will prevent different types of diseases along the way. Knowing what kind to use in each situation will make a difference in how safe and healthy we can stay during this time.

1. When meeting new people

Perk Instant Hand Sanitizer with Moisturizer. This is a good one to help you out after meeting new people and shaking hands. It may feel a little bit strange to whip out some hand sanitizer when you are done meeting someone new, but there are so many germs that others will carry around with them. Turn this into a good ice breaker or a conversation starter and keep your hands safe from all the germs that someone else may bring about.

2. When your hands are a little dry

A common side effect that a lot of people will notice when using hand sanitizer often is that their hands get dry. This is due to the alcohol content inside most sanitizers. And a good choice to help avoid this issue is known as Grove Hydrating Hand Sanitizer. This is a gel that absorbs fast and will feel good on your skin while bringing some good scent and hydration to the hands thanks to the coconut oil that is inside.

3. When you need to eat on the go

Many people during the COVID-19 pandemic will find that they need to eat at home more often. This is one of the best ways to make sure that you can keep yourself safe and healthy because there are fewer germs at home. There are still some situations where you need to eat out, and it is important to keep yourself safe and sound.

When it is time to go out and eat, you can purchase Eat Cleaner Fruit and Veggie Wipes to help you stay safe. These are good wipes that will help you to remove anything bad that is found in your food, including the wax, germs from others touching the food, chemicals, and more. And since they are alcohol-free, you could use them to keep the food clean without adding anything harmful into your body

4. When you need to go on an airplane

Airplane travel has definitely gone down since this pandemic has started, but there are some situations where it just can't be avoided completely. The Clorox Free and Clear Baby Multi-Surface Cleaner Spray and Hard Surface Daily Wipes ca help with this. The CDC recommends that we wipe any public surfaces that we are around, and these wipes will make this easier to do without all the chemicals. These are not necessarily for your hands but can be used to sanitize anything else that you would touch during the day.

5. When on the subway

Everyone can admit that time on the subway is the riskiest part of the day. No matter how far you travel or how long you are on the subway, there are a lot of germs that can be found around us. Between all the different parts of the subway that are touched, all the people who get on from different locations, and more, it is important that we take the time to keep germs away.

Nano Pure Next Generation Hand Sanitizer is a good one to help keep you safe while commuting. You only need to apply it one time, usually before you get on the train, to form a lasting protective layer on the skin. This helps to keep the germs away while you are on the subway, without you needing to go through and spray it nonstop and annoying the other passengers who get on the subway as well.

6. When you go to the gym

Most gyms have been closed in many locations during this time, but now that many are opening up again, it is important to add some sanitation to these areas as well. Zero K Cooling and Cleansing Body and Face Wipes are good to use when you work out. The peppermint oil will help to refresh and cool the body, and then you can use this to help keep your body clean from the germs and can even work for sanitizing the areas where you plan to work out during the day.

7. The office

As you make your way back to the office, there are a lot of germy areas you need to be careful of.

The Byredo Rose Rinse-Free Hand Wash may be a good choice here. It is a great flower scent to use with it so it doesn't smell like you are cleaning all day long You can use it any time that you would like to clean your hands and can't make it to the sink, so use it after touching keyboards, the printer, and anything that is shared in the office.

8. For the beach

If you want to head to the beach and get some good sun after being stuck inside for so long, then Sn Bum Baby Bum Hand Sanitizer is a good option. This company has a lot of products that are highly recommended, even by dermatologists, so we know they are safe even for those with sensitive skin. This is a spray-on sanitizer that you can add to your bag really easily. This way, when you head to the beach, you can sanitize your hands any time that you need to touch something that may have some germs on it.

9. After the beach

If you are worried about all the germs that can be all over you from going to the beach, then it is time to work with Squeaky Clean Antibacterial Hand Sanitizer with Aloe Vera to help you. This is a good one to use because it not only keeps the germs away, but it can help to soothe those sunburns from finally getting into the sun. This aloe vera will help you to get some hydration on your hands and arms while making sure you get rid of all the bad germs that show up at the same time.

10. When it is time for bed

It is important to sanitize yourself before bed. And if you need something with a nice lavender scent that will help you to fall asleep, then Mrs. Meyer's Hand Sanitizer is the right choice. This is a little spritz that you can use and help yourself get rid of the germs and get a soothing scent all at the same time.

Hand sanitizers are a great choice for you to work with. They can make sure that you can kick all of the different germs out, and there are even different mixes that will help you based on the situation you find yourself in at the time. It is usually recommended to go with an alcohol-based hand sanitizer because the alcohol content is good at killing the bacteria and germs right away. Making the right choice in hand sanitizer, whether you choose an alcohol-based or an alcohol-free variety, is important to ensure that we can stop the spread of COVID-19 and other viruses.

Chapter 5:

Disinfectants – The Ins and Outs of Homemade Hand Sanitizers and Disinfectants

There are many hand sanitizers out there to choose from. You can pick from many of those options and see how they work for you. Most of the versions out there are effective and have received FDA approval for being safe to use. The biggest complaint with most is that the alcohol-based versions will dry out your hands and can make them a little uncomfortable.

Another route to go with, whether you want to have full control over the hand sanitizer ingredients or when your area is out of hand sanitizer, and you still need some, is to make your own. There are a lot of great recipes and choices out there that help you to create effective and safe homemade hand sanitizers that can kill bacteria and keep you and your family safe.

Comparing Commercial Hand Sanitizers with Homemade Versions

There are a lot of benefits of working with hand sanitizers. They can be a great alternative when hand washing is not an option, and in between regular hand washing as well. They can kill many bacteria and germs; the specific types are based on the ingredients in the sanitizer you choose (this should be listed on the product you purchase).

Many individuals will choose to work with commercial hand sanitizers. There are many varieties, and they are effective at helping to fight off germs and other viruses. There are many types to choose from in a store or online, allowing you options when it is time to use them to stay safe during this pandemic.

While there are plenty of hand sanitizers to purchase and use from the store, there are many reasons why you may choose to make your own hand sanitizer. There are many reasons why people would go with homemade versions instead of the store-bought versions. Some of the benefits of making your own sanitizers at home include:

1. You can control the ingredients in the sanitizer. While some ingredients work

better than others, when you make your own hand sanitizers, you can pick and choose the ingredients that you want to add in. If you are sensitive to certain ingredients or have an allergy to some, this is easy to remedy with your own solutions.

2. You can make it in bulk. It is possible to make as much hand sanitizer as you would like. It is important to store it well and keep it in a safe space, but it is possible to make a large amount of the hand sanitizer to have nearby when needed.
3. It is a lot cheaper than purchasing at the store. If you make hand sanitizers at home, they often cost a lot less than purchasing the options at the store or online. Whether you want to make it through the high virus season, or when you have a bigger family that goes through a lot of sanitizers, making your own can be more cost-effective.
4. Sometimes, including the beginning of the COVID-19 pandemic, hand sanitizer at the store will run out. This is not an ideal situation, and when we run out, it becomes hard to find the hand sanitizer we need to stay safe. If you can make your own hand sanitizer at home, it is easier to find the ingredients to create these, even when the

store versions of hand sanitizer are gone. This keeps you safe even in uncertain times.

Which Ingredients to Use, and Which to Avoid

There are a lot of simple ingredients that you can use to make sure that you create a safe and effective hand sanitizer at home. In fact, you can make a simple hand sanitizer with some aloe vera gel (the same kind we use to help treat sunburns and other burns), and isopropyl alcohol. The gel will help to thicken the sanitizer, but the type of alcohol you will use is specific. You need it to be 99 percent concentration. If you go with a lower concentration, then it won't be enough to reach that 60 percent that the CDC recommends, and that is necessary for keeping away the germs and killing them.

These are the only two ingredients you need for the most basic hand sanitizer out there, and if those are the only two ingredients that you can find, then that is enough. There are other recipes that you can choose that help to add scents and even moisturizers in case you worry about your hands getting bad and dry along the way. Use natural ingredients that will not lower the effectiveness of alcohol, and you should be good to go.

The most important ingredient is alcohol. This is what most sanitizers use to kill off the bacteria and other germs quickly and efficiently. Without this, the hand sanitizer will not work that well at all. Then there needs to be some medium to use with the alcohol. In the example above, aloe vera was used, there are a few other choices however. If you are using a spray version, then going with water or another liquid that can come out of a spray may be better. If you use a bottle or a pump, then the gel is the best for getting it out and onto your hands.

For the alcohol that you are using, you want to make sure that it will, when mixed, have a ratio of at least 60% alcohol content. Some people think that it is just fine to use a bottle of vodka to clean their hands—and it might be, if all they used was a bottle of 60% vodka. That would require you to get your hands on 120 proof spirits that you might struggle to find. If you can, you can also use Everclear alcohol, which is produced at 60%, 75%, and 95%, meaning that you can get a massive amount of alcohol that is, technically, safe to drink (though not recommended as it takes very little to get drunk enough to start teetering into alcohol poisoning). Keep in mind that, due to the high alcohol content in Everclear, it is actually illegal in many states and you might struggle to actually find it somewhere. You need to be able to improvise, however, and really, isopropyl alcohol will do the job just fine, albeit without the benefit of being able to drink it as well.

Though you can use just straight 60% alcohol to clean your hands, it is not recommended. Very quickly, you will probably discover that your hands become irritated. You need something in your sanitizer that will help to soothe the drying effects of the alcohol. After all, you are not immune to the way that the alcohol works—it kills the germs because of the fact that it dries them out, so it is only natural that the same would happen to your hands as well. To combat this, we typically mix the alcohol with either aloe vera gel or glycerin, both of which are able to help to soothe your hands and fix the problem of drying out.

If you are going to make your own sanitizer, all you need is the sanitizing agent (the alcohol) and the soothing agent to mix in (the glycerin or aloe vera gel). Beyond that, anything else is extra, and anything else will also work to dilute down the alcohol content, which could potentially render your sanitizer useless.

There are a few different ingredients that we need to be careful about. These can show up in commercial hand sanitizers quite a bit, and we need to be careful about adding them into our own homemade versions as well. Some of the ingredients that we should not have in any effective hand sanitizer include:

- **Sodium Lauryl Sulfate**: This is an ingredient linked back to eye and skin irritation. It often damages the cell membranes of your hand and causes more harm than good when it is found inside a hand sanitizer.
- **Parabens**: these are added in to help extend the shelf life of hand sanitizers, but they are known to have effects that disrupt the hormones. These can diminish muscle mass if used too much, and topical versions of it have been detected in tumors of the breast.
- **Ureas**: This is a big cause of contact dermatitis. They will release formaldehyde and can cause heart irregularities, joint pain, and an immune system that is weakened. These are kind of the opposite

of what we want to see with the protection of hand sanitizer, so it is important to avoid them.

- **Synthetic colors:** These will often show up as D&C or FD&C and will be followed by a number and a color. These contain some heavy metal salts that can leave toxins on your skin. They will often cause sensitivity and irritation to the skin.
- **Diethanolamine**: This is a chemical that is linked to cancer, allergies, and even organ system toxicity, so it is best to leave it and anything containing it out of the hand sanitizer you choose.
- **Synthetic fragrances:** There is nothing wrong with adding some fragrance to the hand sanitizer that you make at home. But you need to make sure that you avoid the synthetic versions because of the toxicity levels that they may provide to the body. Make sure to go with versions of fragrances that are real, and that can provide you with additional benefits (such as lavender helping with relaxation).
- **Ethyl alcohol**: This is usually not the best type of alcohol to add to your hand sanitizer, even though it can be effective. The isopropanol version is better to go

with because it is safer, and doesn't cause as many issues to your body.

- **Benzalkonium Chloride**: This is often listed as BAC. It belongs to a group of germicides that are known as "quats" and can be linked back to organ system toxicity, immunotoxicity and allergies, and even cancer.

What to Do if an Allergic Reaction Occurs?

Because of all the benefits that we talked about through this guidebook and how convenient and portable they are, hand sanitizers can be a great way to make sure that we keep away viruses and bacteria and stay safe from COVID-19. Whether you are camping, you are out and about with other people, or something else happens, and you want to sanitize, these hand sanitizers are a great option when hand washing is not possible.

There are times when an individual can have an allergic reaction to a hand sanitizer, or to some of the ingredients that are inside. This often results in a red rash or itchy skin. The good news is that this will often go away and it is not permanent. Ceasing the use of that hand sanitizer will usually be enough to make the allergic reaction go away.

Contact Dermatitis

This is the medical term for an allergic reaction to a substance or a product that is in contact with your skin. Treatment of this is usually going to involve wet compresses, anti-itch creams, and antihistamines, depending on how bad the allergic reaction is. You also want to make sure that you prevent the substance from coming in contact with your skin.

If you come in contact and you find that you do have an allergic reaction, there are a few steps that you can take. First, go and wash the substance from your hands if you just put it on. Some soap and water are often good for this. The rash or itchiness may still be there a bit, though sometimes this does soothe them, this at least stops the substance from causing further damage.

In some cases, washing your hands-off can be enough, and then you simply must stop using that hand sanitizer. If the allergic reaction continues and becomes unbearable, then using the anti-itch cream, antihistamines, and wet compresses until the allergic reaction is gone are the best courses of action to make things easier.

If you do have an allergy to a hand sanitizer, it is a good idea to pick one that has as few chemicals in it as possible. The more chemicals, the more likely that one of them will cause these allergic reactions, or at least cause some irritation. The Environmental Working Group will often advise that individuals should use sanitizers that contain ethanol or ethyl alcohol. Sometimes it is the fragrance in the hand sanitizer that causes the problem so if your skin is already sensitive; it may be best to avoid these types of sanitizers.

For those who have really sensitive skin, you may want to consider wiping the sanitizer off after a few minutes. This is long enough to kill the germs and viruses on your hands and leaves you set to go when you want to do something else, without leaving the chemicals on your hands for too long. You just wipe your hands down with the sanitizer to kill the germs and viruses, and then you wipe off with some wipes as well.

Chapter 6:

Step-By-Step Guide to Making Your Own Hand Sanitizer, Handmade Soap, and Household Wipes

In this chapter, you are not only going to discover why hand sanitizers and other products are good for us in preventing the spread of coronavirus and other similar diseases. You will also take a look at how we can make some of them on our own. These products are so important to the health and wellbeing of the whole country during this time and being able to make some of our own, without having to rely on the store having enough, or even the right kind, can make a big difference.

There are a lot of reasons why people would want to learn how to make some of these products on their own at home. You may be in an area where hand sanitizers ran out, and you were not able to get enough for them or your family. You may be allergic to certain ingredients, and you want to create a sanitizer that works but won't end up harming you or your skin in the process. There are times when you will just want to create hand sanitizer to save money, or to have bulk amounts of it on hand for larger groups or frequent use without running to the store all the time.

There may be many reasons why you would like to make some of these products on your own. No matter the reason, it is important to know how to make them well. The good news is most of these are really simple to make, and you can whip up a big batch, or however much of it you need, in very little time at all. Let's spend some time looking at the steps you can take to create your own hand sanitizer, handmade soaps, and reusable household wipes in no time.

Hand Sanitizer

It is surprisingly easy to make some of our own hand sanitizer without all the hassle, as long as you know what we are doing. And you can make it with just a few ingredients. Of course, there are lots of different recipes out there to try out that add fragrances, moisturizers, and other things to ensure that you get the best out of them. But you can easily make a simple hand sanitizer at home with just a few ingredients.

Making your hand sanitizer is easier than it seems. You only need a few ingredients to get it done. These will include:

1. Rubbing alcohol or isopropyl. This needs to have a 99 percent alcohol volume. If you go for a lower one, you will end up with less than 60 percent alcohol content that is recommended, meaning that it may no longer be effective at neutralizing the viruses that it is attempting to destroy.
2. Aloe vera gel: This helps to add the viscosity that you want to the sanitizer. It also works well to keep the alcohol from evaporating too quickly, which it is likely to do when you are making use of something that is so highly concentrated. Alcohol dissipates on its own, so by combining it with something else, you can slow that process. Even better, aloe vera acts as a great soothing agent to make up for the drying out of your hands that happens when you are constantly coating them in alcohol.
3. An essential oil: This can help give it a different smell that isn't quite so strong of alcohol along the way. Something like lemon juice, lavender oil, or tea tree oil are

good choices though you can choose the one that seems to be the best for you.

The main takeaway that we need to remember when we would like to make our own hand sanitizer, one that is able to get rid of the germs and effectively keep us safe, is to stick with a 2:1 proportion of aloe vera to alcohol. This will make sure that the alcohol content is near the 60 percent that we need compared to the rest of it. If you go off this, then you are not meeting the minimum amount that the CDC recommends to effectively kill most germs.

This is an easy ratio to go with. You can pick any size container that you would like, just make sure that the ratio stays the same. If you have a container that is three cups, you will make two of the cups to fill it alcohol of your choice, and then the other cup would be the aloe vera that we are adding in. And you can go up or down from there, based on how much you would need. This gets harder with some of the smaller amounts, but since many people who make their own hand sanitizer do so to have bulk amounts, this should not be that big of an issue.

Store the hand sanitizer in a safe spot so that it is ready to go. You can even make a big batch and then put it into a smaller container to take on the go with you. Three ingredients are all you need to stay safe, and the third one is not necessary if you want to save some time and money in the process!

Basic Hand Sanitizer Gel

What's inside:

- 99.9% isopropyl alcohol (2/3 cup)
- Aloe vera gel (1/3 cup)
- Essential oils of choice (just a few drops, to add fragrance)

How to make:

1. Measure out your ingredients and add them to a small bowl.
2. Mix the ingredients well to combine thoroughly.
3. Funnel the gel into a bottle, either a squeeze bottle that you can take on the go, or a bottle with the press-down nozzle, for future use.

All you have to do is apply a liberal amount to your hands and then scrub them down accordingly. Remember, the process for sanitizing hands involves you coating them and allowing the alcohol to evaporate off of the skin as you rub it in. Follow these steps:

1. Add a liberal amount to your palm.
2. Rub first palm to palm, coating them both thoroughly in the gel.

3. Then, lace your fingers together, rubbing carefully to get into all of the nooks and crannies.
4. Move to the backs of your hands, scrubbing each for about 5 seconds.
5. Rub your fingernails against your palms, allowing the gel to get into those nooks and crannies as well.
6. Rub your thumb to make sure that it is also getting sanitized, and then switch to the other one.
7. Clean the wrists thoroughly.
8. Continue to rub until your hands are dry. They are now disinfected.

Liquid Hand Sanitizer Spray

If you want to use a liquid hand sanitizer instead of making use of one that is in a thicker gel format, all you would do is substitute the aloe vera gel for glycerin, allowing the glycerin to be the emulsifier instead. This should make it thin enough to allow for the liquid, when mixed with the same ratio, to be used in spray bottles to allow for spritzes on the go instead of gels.

Basic Hand Sanitizer Spray

What's inside:

- 99.9% Isopropyl alcohol (2/3 cup)
- Glycerin (1/3 cup)
- Essential oils of choice (few drops for aroma)

How to make:

1. Mix the ingredients into a bowl until thoroughly blended together.
2. Carefully funnel the ingredients into a spritzer or spray bottle for future use.

To use this, you will simply spritz your hands a few times and then continue to rub them in the same fashion that you would use for the basic hand sanitizer gel. Continue to rub them until you find that your hands have dried, meaning the alcohol has dissipated. Your hands are now clean.

The only real difference between this sanitizer and the previous one is that you have chosen to use a new ingredient to keep your skin from getting irritated. Now, you are using a liquid instead, changing the consistency of the recipe.

Handmade Soaps

Now it is time for you to make some of the hand soaps that you would like. These are a bit more complex than hand sanitizer, but there are hundreds of hand soaps that you can work with depending on the kind that you like. There are different colors, different scents, and different types of handmade soaps that you are able to work with, which can be part of what makes them so much fun.

This section is not going to focus on all of the different soaps that you can make because there are quite a few of them. We are going to take a look at just some simple recipes that you can use to make sure you always have the soap that you would like to be protected. Easy soap recipes that are simple to make, can kill off the germs and will help you use all-natural ingredients can be so important during this time.

One thing to consider when you get started, outside of the basic ingredients we will look at soon, is picking the right kind of mold. There are a few options available for one-pound soap molds. First, the recycled route is a good one. There are a few options that you can use, such as a plastic take away container that you would get when you order some take out. You can easily line the insides with some baking paper, as long as the shiny side is up, and then pour in the soap.

It is also possible to use some paper milk cartons. Make sure to rinse it out and then open the top without cutting it at all. Pour the soap into that top opening and allow it to harden. A few days later, you can rip the paper carton off the soap and get it out. Chop the bar into the right sizes later too.

Many people simply make their own six-bar silicone mold. If you plan to make soap on a regular basis, then you will find that this is an inexpensive way to make sure you make as much soap as you like. A silicone mold will last a long time, and the bars look really nice. On top of that, cutting isn't something that doesn't need to be done.

Now we need to take a look at three easy recipes for soap that we can work with. You can choose which one you like best, or you can find another recipe if that works best for you. But these recipes are designed for beginners, so they are meant to be easy and effective at the same time. All of them should be made at temperatures around 110 degrees. Let's look at a few of the recipes that you can use and see how effective they will be.

Basic Soap

What's inside:

- Essential oil
- Water (.75 c.)
- Lye (.25 c.)
- Palm oil (.66 c.)
- Olive oil (.66 c.)
- Coconut oil (.66 c.)

How to make:

1. Prepare your molds, making sure to cover them with enough plastic to hang over the edge.
2. Combine the coconut oil and the palm oil and then place them into a pot until they start to melt. You can choose different oils if you would like, but they need to be solids and done in the same proportions as one another.
3. While this oil is melting, you can pour the water into a different bowl and then add the lye into this. Always pour solid into the liquid to help reduce the splashes, and there are some heat and fumes here.
4. Stir this mixture until you break the crust on the bottom to make sure it is done well.

You should not notice any granules or anything here.

5. Now it is time to combine the liquid oil. Measure out the olive oil and add it to the solid oils that were melted. You want the temperature to end up around 110 to 120 degrees. Wait if the temperature is higher than this, and consider putting into some ice water if needed.
6. When your mixture is at the right temperature, pour the lye into the pot with the oil. Blend with a blender for about five minutes. You want to find the trace, which is when the soap mixture is thick enough to leave a little trace of itself when you drizzle it on top of your batch.
7. Add in the essential oil of your choice and other herbs or colors if you would like. Then pour this into the prepared mold.
8. Cover the mold with some plastic wrap and add a towel on top to keep all of the heat in. Let it set for a full 24 hours without touching.
9. Once your soap is completely cool, which sometimes takes more than 24 hours, you can cut into thick bars. Allow it to cure for a month in an area that is dust-free before using it.

Easy Foam Soap

What's inside:

- Essential oil of your choice (6 drops)
- Prepared Castile soap (20 percent)
- Water (60 percent)

How to make:

1. Take out a clean jar that can have a soap pump on top of it. Measure out how much "air" needs to be left at the top to make sure you don't overfill this too much.
2. Then take the jar and fill it up about 60 percent with some water.
3. Prepare the Castile soap using the instructions on the package for this. It is going to come undiluted but since we are mixing it with water, it will be fine. You can also make it creamier by replacing five percent of the water with more soap.
4. Add in the essential oil that you would like to use and the soap pump on to the container. Shake to combine and enjoy.

Liquid Soap Gel

What's inside:

- Peppermint or lavender essential oil
- Water (6 c.)
- Castile soap (1 bar)
- Stockpot
- Cheese grater

How to make:

1. Take your bar of soap and grate it with the cheese grater. This will make it a bit easier to get the soap to dissolve in the water later on.
2. Take the water and add it to a pot. Heat it on the stove until it simmers. Measure out two cups of the soap flakes that you worked on and add to the water.
3. Stir to help dissolve the soap in the water. Turn the heat off and then let the soap have some time to dissolve. You can stir a few times, but this will take an hour to finish.
4. If you would like, add in a bit of peppermint or lavender oil to the soap. Allow it to cool down all the way before you put it into your chosen container.

5. This makes 48 ounces of the soap if you are looking for some of the containers that you would like to use along the way.
6. This is a really thin soap, so keep that in mind when you try to pump it out. You can work with a foaming soap bottle. You just fill that bottle halfway with this liquid soap and then add some water to fill it up. This one can also work with your hair or keeping your hands clean!

Reusable Household Wipes

Many people tend to work with household wipes to keep surfaces clean and ready to go. Many of the surfaces that we use and touch can have germs on them too, and commercial wipes can be a quick and easy way to make sure that you are safe and sound from them. It is often better to make your own household wipes that are reusable, though. While the commercial types are useful and convenient, and they do a good job, there are a few reasons why we should avoid using them at all:

1. They are really wasteful. These wipes are only used once before you throw them away. This is bad for the environment. Considering how many we can easily go through during a pandemic or even just the regular flu season, it won't take long before your whole trash can is full of these.
2. They are toxic: These wipes may contain many harsh chemicals that have been shown to provide harmful side effects. They may be good for killing off viruses and bacteria along the way, but they are toxic, and there are better options.
3. They are expensive: Since you can only use each wipe one time and then you have to throw them in the trash. Even a small

cleaning job will need at least a few of these sheets, you are basically just throwing away our money and not getting that many benefits.

Now, there are some commercial wipes that are seen as a little bit safer compared to the other ones. But one thing to remember is that many of these promise to be better, when in fact they are not. Even some of the organic and safer alternatives out there fail when it comes to how good they are for the environment, and they are expensive. There is a much better way that to get the convenience of these wipes without the harmful side effects, the waste and without having to worry about having all those germs around you all the time.

You can make some of your own homemade cleaning wipes. When you see how easy it can be to make these cleaning wipes, you will want to make a whole bunch and keep them around. First, you need to decide on the base for your cleaning wipes. Some people find that old receiving blankets or baby washcloths can work. You can find old fabric or blankets that are thinner at a local thrift shop to keep costs down if you don't have some of these at home. Even old t-shirts will work well for this.

Then you need to find a good container that will let you store all of these wipes and keep them safe. It will depend on what you have available for you. A quart-sized pickle jar can be a good place to start, a mason jar, or any quart-sized container that has a lid you can put on tightly. It is even possible to use some of the old commercial wipe containers, or baby wipes containers to make this work. It is best to stick with the glass containers if you choose to add in some essential oils to the mix because these oils can interact with plastic. But it is up to what you have available at the time.

We can then move on to the homemade cleaning wipes solution. There are a lot of recipes online that you can choose to use to make these. We need to look at something that is quick and simple and can get you effective cleaning. One of the recipes includes:

Homemade Cleaning Wipes

What's inside:

- Thin cloths (20)
- Essential oil of your choice (20 drops)
- Castile soap or a natural dish soap (1 Tbsp.)
- Distilled water (1.5 c.)

How to make:

1. Take out the container that you would like to use and add the soap and the water to it before stirring.
2. If you choose to work with the essential oil, you need to add it into the container at this point.
3. Add the cloths that are already cut up into the container, pressing them down a little bit to help soak up all of the solution.
4. When the cloth is all covered up and ready to go, you can cover the container and flip it upside down to get every inch as well.
5. Store somewhere nice until you need them for quick cleanup sometime during the day.

When it is time to wash these, just throw them in the laundry room and wash like normal. You are only using dish soap and some water, so there isn't anything in here that would make them bad, outside of the germs that you tried to pick up. It is simple and easy to go through, and you are likely to see some amazing results in the process here.

Chapter 7:

Most Effective Types of Medical Face Masks

Along with frequent hand washing and using hand sanitizer on a regular basis, we can also work on wearing face masks to make sure that we are protected, and that we can protect others from getting any germs that we have on ourselves. Since it is possible for us to carry germs and viruses without getting sick, the masks will make sure that we aren't infecting many other people and causing the spread more than before.

There are certain types of masks that we can wear, though. Just because they cover our mouth and our noses doesn't mean that they are effective. Most of us would agree that just putting a random shirt over our face would probably not provide us with a whole lot of protection in the process. So what is the answer here? What is the best kind of face mask? Are there different types of facemasks that we can use? How do we tell which is the best one?

These are all important questions to consider. Picking the right one can make the difference between whether we and our loved ones can stay safe or not. Let's learn a bit more about these face masks and what we can do to keep ourselves safe with the right ones.

Different Types of Masks

There are two main types of masks, surgical masks, and respirators. A surgical mask is going to be a disposable medical device that can be bought in a local pharmacy and will protect against any infections and agents that can be transmitted by droplets. These droplets can include droplets of saliva or secretion from the upper respiratory tract when the wearer exhales.

If this kind of mask is worn by a caregiver, it will protect the patient, as well as the environment that patient is in. If it is worn by the person who is contagious and has the virus or the disease at the time, it will ensure that the patient will not be able to contaminate their surroundings and their environment. You should never wear these masks for more than three to eight hours, depending on the use, and you may need to switch them out more often in some situations.

A surgical mask can also make sure that the wearer is protected from the risk of any splashes of biological fluids. In this case, it is possible that the surgical mask will have a layer that is waterproof. Some of these will be equipped with a visor to help protect your eyes if this situation warrants it.

While there are many situations where these masks can be used, we have to remember that it will not protect against any airborne infectious agents. This means that it is not going to be a good option to make sure that the wearer isn't protected from being contaminated by a virus-like coronavirus.

Then we will find the respirators. These will be the personal protective equipment that someone can wear that will prevent them from inhaling aerosols, including dust, mist, and smoke, and will protect against gases and vapors that can pose harm to the health of the individual. These are not available in the traditional pharmacy, but they can be a good choice to use when you want to be protected against coronavirus or other harmful viruses.

There are two main types of respirators that you may find. These are filtering and insulating. The filtering respirators will consist of a face piece as well as a device for filtering. Sometimes the filter system will be integrated into the face piece that is being used. Depending on the filter, the mask will either be effective just against the particles that come near them or only against vapors and gases.

Filtering respirators are sometimes equipped a bit differently, and it is possible to see them have an exhalation valve to make sure the user is a bit more comfortable. This valve is important because it will make sure there isn't a lot of condensation inside the mask, misting on the glasses, and can help make it easier for the user to breathe while wearing it.

What are the standards?

Each of these mask types will have different regulations and standards that they need to meet, depending on the geographical area of the country. For example, the surgical masks are tested in the direction of exhalation, from the inside to the outside. The tests will take into account how efficient the bacterial filtration is at the time.

In Europe, these surgical masts need to comply with the European Standard that is known as the

EN 14683. This standard has three levels of bacterial filtration efficiency, which are known as BFE1, BFE2, and Type R. Things are a little different in the United States, where the surgical masks need to respect the ASTM standards. These also provide us with three levels of protection from the low risk of exposure to fluids to the higher risk of exposure along the way.

There are also standards for the respirators as well. These are tested going from the direction of inspiration, so they go from outside to inside. There are three classes of these disposable respirators that we can use, and they include:

- FFP1: These will have the least amount of filtering of the three masks. The aerosol filtration needs to be at least 80 percent, and the leakage that gets inside can be a maximum of 22 percent. This mask is more used as a dust mask at home or when you would like to do some home renovation kind of things.
- FFP1: These will be a bit better at filtering while you work. They come with a minimum of 94 percent filtration and a maximum of 8 percent leakage inside. They are often used in agriculture, construction, and even healthcare

professionals will rely on them quite a bit. They are good for protecting against influenza and are the current option for coronavirus and other similar issues.

- FFP3. These masts provide you with the most filtering. The minimum filtration percentage is at least 99 percent, and the maximum amount of leakage that is allowed will be 2 percent. They will be good to use against some very fine particles, including asbestos.

The United States has a few different options when it is time to keep people safe from the different viruses that are out there. These will be similar to what we see above with the European options, but there are a few differences that will show up here. Some of the things that we will see include:

1. Class N: These are the ones that will have no oil resistance. A distinction will be made between the N95, N99, and N100. The number that comes after our letter will tell us the percentage of filtration of suspended particles that can get in based on the type of mask that we are using.
2. Class R: This is a type of mask that is resistant to oil for eight hours or less. The

distinction will be similar, but we will use R95, R99, and R100 instead.

3. Class P: These are the masks that are completely resistant to oil without any kind of variations.

As we can see, there are a lot of different types of masks out there that we are able to use. Figuring out the right one for your needs, and the right one that will ensure you take proper care of ourselves during a pandemic, or even during a normal flu can be a difficult task. While many people do not wear masks on a regular basis, the spread of coronavirus and some of the different things that have led to this virus spreading so much has shown us just why these masks are so important in the first place.

Which Masks are Best for Protection?

Now that we know a little bit more about the different types of masks that are out there, we need to explore more about the types of masks that each person should wear, and discuss which ones are the best for providing protection. To start, we need to look at what you should do the second you suspect you are contagious. As soon as a you realizes that you may be sick, you need to start wearing a surgical mask any time you go out in public or are around other people to stop the virus from spreading.

In Europe, it is necessary for caregivers to wear masks as well. This is just as much for keeping the patient safe as it is for making sure the caregiver doesn't get sick. This caregiver in Europe will need to wear a respirator mask that is at least FFP2 or FFP3 to stay safe.

The rules are a bit different in the United States. The requirement here is the N95 respirator filter for 95 percent of airborne particles. This mask is able to help filter out the viruses and bacteria according to the CDC. Caregivers need to use a mask if they are around someone who is sick, but they can choose any of the three classes of respirators based on what they like and how much protection they want.

Which is Better: Reusable or Disposable Masks?

The next thing that we need to look at is whether it is better to use a disposable mask or a reusable mask? These both have benefits as the reusable mask will save money, and as long as you clean it off regularly, you will be able to go out in public and keep yourself and others safe the whole time. On the other hand, disposable masks are nice because you never have to worry about washing them as time goes on.

Surgical masks are an example of disposable medical devices, which means that you need to dispose them properly after you use them. Depending on the respirator that you use, it can be reusable or disposable. If you have a respirator that is reusable, make sure to watch the filter and replace it any time it gets full, or the mask will not work as well for you.

The effective life of either one of these two masks is going to vary depending on the use. For general-purpose, this can range from three hours to eight, depending on the concentration of the contaminant, the temperature, the humidity, the volume of the air breathed, and more. If you are outside in your own yard gardening and a few neighbors are out, and the air is nice and cool, then you can wear the mask longer than if you head to the local clinic for a checkup. Wearing a face shield over the mask is a good way to prolong how the time you can wear the mask for.

Chapter 8:

Everything You Need to Know About Homemade Face Masks

Now it is time for us to take a look at making some of our own masks at home. There are a lot of different types of masks, and we explored a few of the common ones that you can purchase. If you want to go with one of those, then there is no problem with that. But since most of them are expensive, you may have to throw them out after each use, and it is hard to get one that will fit directly to your face, it is sometimes beneficial to make our own face masks along the way.

In this chapter, we are going to explore some of the components that we need to consider homemade masks. You want to make sure that you are picking out material and more that not only fits your face and looks good but will also protect you along the way. There are lots of materials to work with, but not all of them will provide the protection that you are looking for. With this in mind, let's take a look at a few considerations to remember when it comes to making your own homemade face masks before we dive into the final chapter and learn how to actually create these masks.

Why You Should Make Your Own Face Mask

There are a number of reasons why someone may choose to make their own face mask instead of purchasing one that is available at the store. Some of the reasons why someone would want to make their own face masks to keep them protected against coronavirus include:

1. They are easy and fun to make: As you can see with a simple search, there are lots of different ways that you can make your own masks. This is part of the fun. You can find the pattern and the steps that fit best for you and then create something that is a lot of fun.
2. You can personalize them based on what fits you. The masks that you find at the store are often boring and plain white. When you make some of your own, you can pick out the material that makes the best sense for you and move on from there.
3. If there are limited supplies of face masks in your area, you still have something to keep you safe. With how quickly the coronavirus spread around, it didn't take long before all

of the masks were gone as well. This made it hard to find the supplies that are necessary to purchase your own. When you make some of your own masks, you never have to worry about the supply and demand of these masks because you can just make your own.

4. They are easy to clean and can be reused as often as you want. Since you are using cloth, you can easily clean these up and reuse them as many times as you would like. That makes them versatile and easy to work with compared to some of the other disposable options.
5. They cost less than other masks. You can sometimes use materials that are found around your home. If this is something you can do, then the masks will cost very little, much less than the disposable ones that most people choose to go with.
6. They are effective at keeping you safe and sound: Even though they are made at home, as long as you design and wear these masks well, you will find that they are really effective at keeping away coronavirus and other viruses. When you make them well, which we will show you soon, you will have some amazing protection.

As we can see, there are a lot of benefits to working with your own homemade masks, and it is worth your time to figure out how to make them, and how to get them to fit for your needs. Let's learn a little bit more about them, and then we will dive into the steps you need to create your own masks in no time.

The Best Materials to Use

A surgical mask that doesn't meet the N95 requirement will only be able to filter out about sixty to sixty-five percent of the particles. This is pretty standard for this kind of mask, so there isn't necessarily one that is better than the others. With this in mind, you are able to double up something like flannel pajamas or a pillowcase and still make a mask that will provide you with this amount of filtration and protection. Between this and the light test, it is easier to figure out how well a material is able to filter.

What is the light test? You just take the material and hold it up to a light. If you are able to see the light through the fabric pretty well, then this is not as good of a material to use for your mask. If the light can get through easily, then so can all the viruses and germs that you are trying to protect yourself. The thicker and the denser the material, while still being breathable and not causing you to not get enough air, the better.

This makes cotton a really good option to work with if you need to stick with something already around the house. According to the CDC, it is recommended that you take two layers of tightly woven 100 percent cotton fabric to help with this. A bedsheet with a high thread count or some quilter's material are the best two options for this.

Researchers at Wake University took some time to test out the different masks that were provided by community volunteers and found two options that seemed to work the best when it came to protection. The first option is a double layer of cotton that had a thread count of no less than 180. Then there was the two-layer mask that had the outer layer with regular cotton and then an inner layer that had flannel.

While having two layers is not necessarily a bad thing, we do need to be careful. The more layers, the more filtration protection, but then we run into issues with not being able to breathe while wearing the items either. You want to make sure that you can breathe comfortably through your nose when you wear the mask. Sticky nose hairs can be a good way to catch some of the particles that get through the masks and protect you before they get further into your lungs. If you make a mask that is not porous enough, then you will start to breathe around the sides of the masks, instead of breathing through it, which is defeating the point here.

For example, vacuum bags can be really hard to breathe. And then some of these will also contain fibers and fiberglass that you should not want to inhale in the first place. They will help prevent some of the filtrations that you want, but you will breathe things in that are bad for you, so this can cause an issue.

There were a few researchers at Cambridge University who wanted to compare the breathability and the filtration of the different mask materials that are used in homemade masks. They found that masks that are made out of cotton T-shirts or pillowcases seemed to get the best balance between breathability and filtration, so those are good materials to use.

Things like linen, pillowcases, silk, t-shirts made out of cotton, quilters cotton, and scarves are on the more breathable side while still allowing a good amount of filtration. They are not at 100 percent, but neither are more surgical masks. On the other hand, we want to avoid a few different materials because they can cause problems. Things like an antimicrobial pillowcase, a cotton and polyester blend, a tea towel, or a vacuum cleaner bag are all less breathable and probably not the best choices to use here.

Why Use a Filter?

Although pillowcases and cotton tea towels are effective for face masks, there is research out there that suggests how important filters can be as well. For example, an assistant professor at Missouri University of Science and Technology, Yang Wang, told The New York Times this week that the use of filters will promote safe breathing and will make sure that any particles in the air can be removed properly.

However, the placement of the filter is going to matter as well. And replacing that filter often is critical to getting it to work well for you. Filters have to be placed right between the two layers of fabric that you use with your mask to make sure that they work while preventing you from inhaling the materials that are part of the filter.

Any of the filter materials that you use, whether we work with polypropylene or HEPA, need to be right between two additional layers of fabric. It can be any of the fabric choices that you would like, such as nylon, silk, or cotton, to make sure that you are not inhaling any of the materials that are found in the filter. These can sometimes be abrasive and hard on the lungs, so putting all of the filters between the parts of the mask can help protect you.

Another thing to consider when you are picking out the filter that you want to use is to pick out a fabric for the filter that will not extrude high amounts of fiber and other synthetic materials. This is because inhaling that glass fiber, which is found in some filter fabric, can cause a variety of respiratory diseases in humans. Since we are using these as a way to protect ourselves against respiratory disease in the first place, it is important to avoid this issue.

Of course, we always want to go with a fabric that will allow for clear, unobstructed breathing, one that is not going to saturate that easy with moisture, and one that will not give us a ton of fiber or other synthetic materials because we do not want to inhale these. There are many filters out there; we just need to do our research and figure out which ones are the best for our health.

While just making sure you use the right kind of material and making sure that it doesn't let in light during the light test will be enough in most cases, some individuals will choose to work with a filter in their masks. This can be an added layer of protection and is useful for those who need to be out with the public, and out around a lot of other people during the pandemic.

It is up to you whether you would like to use the filter. If you plan to be out and about for prolonged periods of time, adding a filter into your mask is going to be one of the best ways to keep the bad stuff out while keeping you nice and safe along the way. This helps you to still breathe well when you wear the mask while providing a bit more protection. Most homemade masks will provide about 60 percent protection, which is a lot better than going without one, but there are some situations where you will need more, and adding the filter in will help.

If you plan to just go out on occasion or you want to wear the mask just when you are around other friends and family, then the filter may not be necessary. Many times the filtering that comes naturally with some of these face masks will be enough to keep you safe and sound during the pandemic.

For those who decide that using the filter is the best option, there are lots of patterns out there that will show you how to add the filter in. Sometimes it is a special piece of equipment that you need to work with, and other times it may just be an additional layer of cloth in your mask. You can pick the option that works best for you.

HEPA vacuum filters

One option that is of really good help when making a mask filter is the HEPA vacuum filters. They have a high-efficiency label when it comes to filtering out small particles. This includes many of the droplets that are responsible for much of the respiratory virus transmission. They are breathable, easy to get, and they don't have a lot of those harmful synthetic materials that we need to worry about.

If you don't have one of these filters ready to go, then you can include the HEPA vacuum bags in your mask, following some of the same rules as we had before. You just need to make sure that any bag that you use, even the HEPA bags, does not have dangerous materials. The gold standard, though, is HEPA, so you may want to just save some time and work with them. If you can't find these, then an air conditioner filter works well too.

Alternate Face Masks

There are a lot of alternate forms of masks that we can use to make sure that we are able to keep the virus away and to help us to not spread the virus to other people. The cloth masks that use cotton, especially quilter's cotton, are the best to use because these ensure that the face is protected, provide a good level of filtration, especially if you use two layers and add a filter in, and are still breathable. There are several other options that we can choose to work with, including:

Cloth Masks

This depends on what kind of face mask you are trying to work with. Many times these are not going to be thick enough unless you do the light test that we talked about before. Most of the items that we consider cloth are easy to breathe through, which can be nice, but they are not going to protect against some of the ways that the virus can be spread between one side to the next. These also get wet from saliva easily so that is going to make the problem even worse.

Plastic Sheet Shield mask

These often go over the head like a visor and will be used in addition to a regular mask. The point of these is to add in an added layer of protection, though sometimes they can be used on their own. It is like a plastic screen that goes in front of the whole face, and not just over the mouth and the nose. These are a bit easier to wear compared to some of the others, and they allow for easier breathing since they are not right up against the mouth. There is still some worry that these will not provide the protection that is necessary, so they aren't really the best option.

Scuba Face Mask

Some people have resorted to working with a scuba face mask to help get things done. This is one option if you are short on supplies, but it is not recommended in most cases. It will cover the face and the mouth so you know you will stay protected from the virus, and, likely, you will not spread it around either. There are some issues here, though, because scuba masks are not really designed to be used this way. They are made to help you breathe under the water, and not out in the open around other people. The protection is going to be minimal and har to breath in when you don't get to rely on an oxygen tank, so they are not the best option to use at all.

Wet Wipe Masks

We spent some time before talking about how to make your own wet wipes and how easy they can be. And since they will use random cloth and t-shirts and more from around the house, they seem like a good idea. When you add in that they have sanitizing solutions on them, then many wonder if this is the solution that they are looking for.

There are a few things to consider here. Depending on the material that you decide to use, you should be fine wearing the mask and staying protected. Keep in mind that if you use wet wipes, then the masks are going to be wet near your face, and that is not an enjoyable experience. If you go with the wrong kind of material here and you don't pick one that is thick enough and has a good enough filtration system, then they are not going to work well at all. There has to be a good mixture and we have to make sure that we pick out the right types and be careful about how wet these actually are when we make them.

Bandana masks

Working with a bandana mask seems like the perfect idea. This is a simple process that would make it easy to put something on really quickly without having to put it all together and hoping that it will work out for you later on. You can just grab a bandana, put it on around your head, and call it good. This is a quick and efficient way to get yourself covered and make sure that you are prepared when you go out in public.

There are a few things to consider when you work with the bandana mask, though. These usually are not very thick. There are a few exceptions, and if you fold the bandana over and do the light test and it works, then this is a lot better. But many of the bandanas that you will use will lack this thickness, and that makes them inefficient with the work. They also don't hook behind the ears, which can make it harder to keep them in place. It would be nice for this to work all of the time, but there are a few problems that take the bandana, though it would be really easy to work with, out of the running.

Cotton Face Masks

For the most part, a cotton mask is going to be one of the best choices to use here. They are lightweight while still passing the filtration system, and you can use any of the materials that you would like along the way. Even a nice t-shirt or some extra quilter's fabric that is lying around will work to make this one happen. It is easy, it is breathable, so you don't have to worry about that, and they are still going to provide you with the filtration that you need. Or, you can add in an added level of filtration if this is what you need as well.

Most of the masks that you will find online will be made out of cotton material. Because of the reasons above and the fact that the CDC even recommends these, it is no wonder that these are the most popular masks that you will find on a regular basis.

Flannel Masks

We can also work with flannel a little bit to help us make some of the masks that we need. This material is a little bit thicker than some of the others so that can make it less preferable than cotton. But it definitely passes the filtration test, so that will be nice if you are looking for a mask that will fit your needs. Sometimes the filtration is too thick, though, and breathing into flannel is not as comfortable or as enjoyable as we will see with cotton or some of the other choices out there.

One thing that we did explore earlier, and which you can do when making your own masks at home as well, is that when flannel and cotton are mixed together, you can make some of the best masks. This gives you some of the filtration benefits that you can get with the flannel and the breathability that you can get with the cotton and gives it all to you in one package.

Filter Bag Masks

It is usually not recommended to use a filter bag masks. These may sound like a good idea because they come right with the filter that you would like. But they are thick and hard to breathe in. And unless you are able to get them specially made to make sure they fit in with some of the regulations out there, they may not provide you with all of the protection that you want.

With this said, it is really useful to add a filter to some of the masks that you create. And these filter bags can be just the thing that you need to make the filters in any of the other masks that we have talked about. If you feel that you need a good filter in your mask to keep you and others protected a bit better, then add one of these into the mix as well.

As we can see, there are a lot of options when it is time to make your own mask at home. It often depends on what you are interested in, which one you think will provide you with the most protection, and what will keep you comfortable while you are out and about.

Chapter 9:

3 Step-By-Step Guides to Making Your Own Reusable Medical Face Masks

Now, we have spent plenty of time talking about the benefits of wearing face masks and making sure that you can protect yourself as much as possible. It is time to start looking at how to make them yourself as well. Thankfully, the process of making your mask is not very difficult—anyone can learn to do it, so long as you have some basic knowledge of sewing. While it can help to be able to sew well, and while having a sewing machine will absolutely speed things along, you can get by so long as you can thread a needle and follow some basic instructions.

We will take a look at how to make a face mask that will work first with elastic loops around the ears. This is a great option if you want something quick, easy, and is not likely to fall off if you are not careful. However, if you want something that is more secure and more in line with recommendations to allow for that perfect custom fit, you will want to use ties instead, and we will discuss that as well.

As you read through these guides, you will see points during which it is recommended that you take additional steps. For example, we will discuss how to create pockets for filters, but if you prefer, you can skip this entirely and just have the layers of fabric itself. We will take the time to consider how to fit the mask to your face with the use of wiring as well to allow you to create that nice, tight seal right around the nose. This will give you the best chance at preventing any transference of droplets that could lead to transmission of disease.

These masks can be altered easily and we will go over how you can make them in both kid-friendly sizes with just a few quick shifts to the measurements, meaning that you are able to protect your entire family with ease. All you have to do is make sure that your masks are measured out. In addition, you will learn about some of the simple changes that you can make along the way to make sure that your mask is as secure as possible. You can customize your mask nearly endlessly with these sorts of options, from changing the type of fixtures to adding pockets or pleats or even nosepieces to help the fit.

Before we get into the steps of making a mask, let's discuss the importance of measurements right now—your mask needs to be snug. It needs to fit well and to have a solid placement on the face to protect the wearer. This means that you don't want to just eyeball the measurements. Just kind of guessing what to cut out can cause you problems with having not enough coverage or having a mask that is just too big to really be useful. By following the measurements that you will be provided to a T, you know that you will have just the right amount of give for your margins. You will have leeway for your sewing so that everything will fit together well. You will know that the mask will fit most people if you can follow them accordingly.

Now, let's begin and start working on masks that will help you and your loved ones avoid the viruses and illnesses going around as much as possible!

Elastic Loop Mask

The first mask that we will consider is a flat fabric mask that is sewn with elastic ear loops. If you wanted to, you could also consider altering the way that you attach the elastic as well so that instead of resting on the ears, it could go alongside the back of the head by shifting the loops to be attached so that one end of elastic is on a left hand corner while the other end is on the right hand corner. When you do this on both corners, you now have a mask that you can slip right over your head instead.

With that note and alteration aside, let's take a look at the steps to beginning your mask.

Step 1: Measurements

The beginning of this process is measuring everything out and creating your templates. If you will be making more than one mask, it helps to create a paper template that you can use so you only have to do the measurements once. When you have the template, you can place it onto the back of your fabric and then mark where you will be cutting without having to break out the ruler every single time that you are measuring out fabric. Considering that you will have to do, at minimum, two layers of fabric, having a template is one of the best things that you can do. In particular, making your template out of cardstock or thick paper will be the most stable for you to use again and again.

The template should have the following measurements:

- **Child sized:** 4 inches x 6 inches
- **Adult sized:** 6 inches x 12 inches

Measure your rectangles with those dimensions and then cut them and set aside.

Step 2: Cutting the Fabric

When it is time to start sewing, you want to first get two strips of fabric that will match the dimensions of the templates you created. This allows you to create a mask that is layered with the right measurements so that they are aligned properly.

To measure the fabric for cutting, you will simply put your template onto your fabric, pinning it in place if you choose to do so for more accuracy. Then, either cut along the template itself, or you can also choose to trace with a pen on the fabric to mark the lines that you will need to cut. Either option works.

Using scissors for fabric, carefully cut out your rectangles of fabric as straight as you can. You want to make sure that it is able to line up easily. It is okay if it is not exact—but it should be as close as possible to work well.

Step 3: Elastic

Next, you will want to measure out your elastic ties as well. You will not want to use too much—remember, it is the tension from the elastic that keeps the strips in place and will allow you to create the right shape in the first place. Ultimately, the types of elastic can vary. For the most part, however, 1/8 braided elastic is what is recommended for use in homemade face masks. In a pinch, you can also make use of taking a hair tie and cutting it, then sealing it accordingly. If you don't have elastic, however, don't worry too much—you can also make use of the tied mask, which we will be talking about shortly. You will want the following measurements:

- **Child-sized:** 5 inches each for ear loops; not recommended to use over-head for young children
- **Adult-sized:** 7 inches each (one per side) for ear loops, or 12-14 inches each if going for a pullover mask

Step 4: Sewing

When you have everything all prepared, it is time to start sewing, whether you choose to do so by hand or by other means. To do so, you need to align everything just right. Make sure that your rectangles of fabric are aligned and sew together tightly. You want to make sure to go along all four sides with a clearance of roughly .25 to .5 inches away from the edge.

With the initial round of sewing done, prepare your ties, whether elastic loops or fabric. Place them in the corners, where your sewing is the tightest, and attach. Then, sew them in as well.

Step 5: Securing

Finally, it is time to secure the whole thing. You want your mask to be as tight as possible; you don't want it to be able to fall apart on you, and for that reason, you need to make it a point to do an extra row of stitching for good measure. This will ensure that you have sealed the two pieces of fabric together closely, and you also give your ties an extra layer of protection as well. Give a second pass in the sewing machine or by hand in roughly the same distance all the way around.

Optional third layer

If you want to really secure your mask and make sure that it will be safe for you to use, you can make use of a third layer. When you add in a third layer to the mask, you will make it harder for the viruses and other particulates in the air to get through them. In particular, you will want to make use of flannel if you want to add in a third layer—it has been found to be highly effective on its own. While you cannot get the same effectivity of an N-95 mask when you make use of just fabric, you can up the percentage of effectiveness of the mask itself.

To add in a third layer is really as simple as it sounds—you would just sew an extra layer of fabric, cut to the same parameters, to the mix. It won't require you to do much at all.

Optional flipping inside out

If you preferred, or if you wanted to add in a pocket to your mask, you could choose to sew with the outside of your fabric facing toward itself inwardly, creating an inside-out mask while only sewing along three of the four edges when you first make your mask. By leaving that fourth edge open to allow for the mask to be flipped, you will be able to hide all of your raw edges. It can help the mask to stick together longer just because of the way that it will work and it will look nicer as well. You would simply flip the mask inside out and continue assembly at that point, allowing you to continue on with the edges hidden.

You can even leave that opening in the mask and use it as a place in which you can add an optional filter layer to help to up the effectiveness of the mask.

Optional nosepiece

Similarly, if you wanted to add in a nosepiece, you would simply leave one of the four sides open when you first sewed the fabric together, then add the wire to place in the top of the mask. At that point, you would sew the wire into place on all sides to keep it firmly secured. Then, you just make it a point to sew up that fourth side and continue on without any problems.

Creating Ties for Masks

If you don't want to use elastic, or you find that your elastic isn't quite the right fit or is uncomfortable for any reason, you have some simple solutions that can help you to create the alterations that you need. Creating fabric ties that you can use to make your mask endlessly adjustable is something that is quite simple to do—all you have to do is make sure that you can sew somehow, or you can choose to use materials that won't require .

These ties can be substituted right in where you would normally add the elastic onto your mask, meaning that you can add these to any of the mask patterns that you are provided in this chapter. To make these is quite simple, and you can even get creative with them—you can make them in complementary colors so that they can create a nice and fashionable accent to your mask.

If you do not want to go through the effort of sewing these, note that you can make use of just about anything else that is long, thin, and able to be tied. From shoelaces to ribbons, if you can tie it securely, it will do just fine as your substitute for your ties. Now, let's go over the process of making fabric ties. Keep in mind that you can use these ties on both child-sized and adult masks just fine, and you will need four of the ties for every mask that you make—one for each corner.

Step 1: Measure

Start by measuring out your strips of fabric. You want strips of 1.5" by 20" to give you plenty of clearance for your masks. This means that they should fit a wide array of different people, large and small, without a problem.

Step 2: Fold

Next, you need to fold and sew to protect your edges first. At one end of the strip, you need to take in about .25" of length, folding it so the outside is out and the inside of the fabric, if patterned is touching inside fabric. You will then attach it so that it cannot detach while folding. This allows you to know that your ends are not raw and therefore won't fray or cause you problems. The second end of the fabric is left raw to be secured into the face mask.

Now, with the bottom of the fabric facing upward, you want to fold in the strips to make sure that they are secure. This will also hide the edges and reinforce them. To do this, you will take one of the long ends and fold it into the center of the fabric along the entire length. Repeat with the bottom side. This should leave you with a sort of tube of fabric, with one seam that is open in the middle. Now, fold the entire strip of fabric at that seam, securing it. Your ties are now effectively layered four times over.

Step 3: Sew

Finally, you must sew the entire fabric strip along the side. This should hide the ends nicely, creating a firm and aesthetically pleasing look to the ties. As you sew, you will probably want to secure the folds along the way so that they are not constantly coming undone.

When your strips are done, make it a point to sew them, raw side against the mask according to the instructions for the mask pattern that you are using.

Pleated Masks

Some people prefer to pleat their masks—this allows for the mask to curve better to the face, mimicking the form of masks used by surgeons. Typically, when you make use of a pleated mask, you need to create a mask that is flipped inside-out, but this also allows for the edges to be much neater and the seam will be hidden in this mask. Let's take a look at the instructions for this as well:

Step 1: Measure and make templates

Begin by preparing all of your measurements and templates out of paper. This particular template only requires you to use one rectangle of fabric instead of two, folding them together instead of cutting two and securing them. You will need the following:

Adult masks

- One rectangle 16 inches by 8.5 inches
- Four ties or two pieces of elastic, depending upon preference

Child masks

- One rectangle 14 inches by 6.5 inches
- Four ties or two pieces of elastic, depending upon preference

Step 2: Fold and sew

Next comes the basic assembly. You must fold the fabric in half, with the outside of the fabric (the patterned side) facing inward. Then, along the topmost edge, opposite of the fold, need to sew, leaving a 4-inch opening that will serve as the pocket in the mask. This opening is large enough for the addition of an additional filter if you choose to add one to the mask, though that is optional.

When you sew this, you want to make use of a 5/8" seam allowance to allow for the seam to hold when you invert the mask. Remember, the whole point of this is to allow for your filter pocket, as well as so you can turn the mask the right way. Even if you are foregoing the filter pocket, you want to make sure that this opening is here so that you can turn the masks the right way.

Step 3: Flip and sew

Now, you want to change the fold so that instead of the opening being on one of the edges, it is centered in the middle of the fabric panel instead. Press down flat to center it and then use an iron to open the seam. You then want to fold so that the excess seam allowance is sealed, allowing you to finish the edge and keep things nice and neat, allowing for the removal of filters if necessary.

Step 4: Attaching the ties

Whether you are using elastic or ties, you will follow the same process. The only difference is that you will use four ties instead of just two elastic pieces. Pin each of your into place in the corners. Make sure that your looped ties are on the same side of each other. They should be affixed roughly .5 inches from the edges.

You want to sandwich the loops or elastic between the two layers of fabric, as they will be turned inside out to face the right way. Make sure that you carefully affix the loops with pins so that you can make sure that they are just right into the mask, such as in the picture below.

Step 5: Securing the ties and sides

Now comes working on the sides of the mask. Keep in mind that if you mess up here, you will accidentally secure your ties or elastic—they have to be out of the way of the stitches or you will have problems later on. Secure them first where they are pinned with the use of backstitching to ensure that they won't get stuck.

Then, you need to also sew the sides of the mask as well. You want to make sure that you continue to leave some seam allowance so that it can be inverted. In particular, aim for roughly 3/8 inches of allowance for the inversion. When that is done, consider trimming up the corners without clipping the stitches—it helps with the inversion process.

Step 6: Flip the mask and press it

Next comes flipping out the mask so that it can be finished up. You're almost done! Here, you want to carefully turn the mask to be right side out. If the corners don't want to pop out all of the way, you can make use of the back of a pen or a chopstick or another long, thin stick to push out the corners completely. Then, when it is all oriented the right way, iron it out. This will allow you to get that nice, crisp look at the seams.

Step 7: Adding a nosepiece

Next comes adding a nosepiece. While optional, it is highly recommended so that you can make sure that your mask will secure appropriately to your face. This is typically done so that you can get a better seal overall. Some people make use of pipe cleaners while others prefer floral wire.

These options are all highly effective; they will work to ensure that you can bend it to fit but also won't make it impossible to work with. The only problem is you will want to be mindful of the material and make sure that it can withstand the washing process. Make sure that wire is bent inward toward itself to protect the fabric from being poked through.

To secure the nosepiece, you will want to put it in through the pocket hole and then push it all the way up to the top of the mask. It should rest between the two top strips of ties or the three top elastic strips. When in place, you will then want to sew it into place around all three sides. This will secure it into place firmly and allow you to avoid running into problems with it slipping around later on.

Step 8: Pleating the mask

You should be putting in three pleats to the mask as well to create that nice fit. To do this, you can choose to measure out the sides and mark them at even increments so that you can fold it accordingly. You want three pleats spaced .5 inches apart. Then, fold the pleats into place and pin them so that they will fit neatly and ensure that they are all facing the same direction, with them pointing away from where you added the wire to ensure that the pleats will be downward when worn. When your pleats are right where you want them, iron them down. Then, sew along the sides once more to make sure that it is fully secured. Be mindful of the elastic or the ties during this process–you don't want to accidentally secure them somewhere that they shouldn't be.

Ideally, you will sew along the edge two or three times to completely secure it. And that's it! Your mask is ready for you to add in the filter material of your choice.

Conclusion

Thank you for reading *Protect Yourself From Viruses*. The next step is to get started with protecting yourself against coronavirus and any of the other bad infections and viruses that are out there. This guidebook focused on some of the big concerns about viruses that can come out during any time of the year, whether we are talking about the new COVID-19 or any of the flu viruses that have gone around in the past. It is important to be protected and to understand that while a vaccine can make things easier, it takes a lot of time and is not going to be a quick fix for us at all. In the meantime, since it may take years, we need to find some good solutions that will keep us safe.

The good news is that the most effective solutions that will keep us safe during coronavirus and any other virus that seems to come along in the past or the future are often the easiest. We have found that wearing a mask when out in public, keeping some distance, and washing hands, either with soap and water or hand sanitizer, can be enough to keep us from getting sick and can stop the spread of the virus along the way.

This guidebook took some time to explore all of the different parts of staying safe and healthy that you need to know. There is hope, and there are easy methods that will help keep coronavirus away, no matter how bad the whole situation may seem in the process. The simple steps that we talked about in this guidebook are definitely enough to help you stay safe and feel your best, even in the middle of the pandemic.

In this guidebook, we spent some time talking about a lot of really important topics that will make a difference in how we are able to stay safe and how we can stop the spread of virusses. Many people assume that all hope is lost until a vaccine is released, but as we learned from the WHO, the CDC, and from this guidebook, simply disinfecting the surfaces around you, using hand sanitizer or washing your hands, and wearing face masks is enough to keep ourselves and those around us safe! While a vaccine would be nice, we have an arsenal of tools that we can use that are just as effective as well.

Some of the different topics that we explored in this guidebook to help us prepare for fighting off not just COVID-19, but also any other virus that finds us, includes:

1. Understanding how bacteria and viruses work and how they are able to affect the body and make us sick.
2. The guidelines that the WHO and CDC provide to us to stay safe, even in the middle of this pandemic, to ensure that you can stay healthy and that you don't spread around the virus, even if you don't experience the symptoms yourself.
3. The importance of handwashing and how to use hand sanitizers, when they are made properly, how they are able to help keep us safe and kill bacteria. We even explored some of the ways to make your own soaps and hand sanitizers, so you never have an excuse not to be safe again.
4. A look at how masks actually work to protect us against the coronavirus and other viruses, and how to make some of our own if the materials and the supplies are not readily available at the store.

And this is just the beginning, So many people were caught off guard when COVID-19 started to show up, and many were not sure how to respond or how they could prevent the spread. This guidebook showed you the exact steps that you could take to fight the virus and stop its spread. We looked at how the process of a vaccine works, and while there is hope that one will come out at some point, that may be several years or more in the future. This guidebook showed you how you can protect yourself here and now against the virus, rather than sitting around waiting for a vaccine that will come too late.

My goal through this guidebook is that you can see that while a pandemic makes us feel out of control and like things are going downhill fast, there are actually quite a few things that you can control. You can socially distance from others and keep your meetings and errands just to those that are critical. You can wear a mask when you take care of someone or when you plan to go out and about. And you can even wash your hands frequently and use hand sanitizer in between. All of these are relatively simple ideas, but they work to keep us all protected.

We have the power to take control over whether we get sick, or even whether we spread the disease to other people around us. Taking our health into our control and using some of the steps that are listed in this guidebook will make it so much easier for us to stay safe and keep others safe along the way as well. When you are ready to fight off COVID-19 and any other virus that is out there, make sure to check out this guidebook and see how relatively easy it can be.

Finally, if you found this book useful in any way, a review on Amazon is always appreciated!

Resources

8 Krazy Uses for Hand Sanitizer. (2019). Retrieved from https://thekrazycouponlady.com/tips/at-home/8-krazy-uses-for-hand-sanitizer

Alcohol-Based Vs Alcohol-Free Hand Sanitizer. (2020, May 16). Retrieved from https://www.cupidlimited.com/blog/alcohol-based-vs-alcohol-free-hand-sanitizer/

American Safety Council. (2015). Myths About Hand Sanitizer. Retrieved from https://blog.americansafetycouncil.com/myths-about-hand-sanitizer/

Annis, F. (2013, October 29). Why Wearing A Face Mask Is Important - Universal Medical Inc. Retrieved from https://blog.universalmedicalinc.com/wearing-face-mask-important/

B. (2020, May 19). START HERE! Retrieved from https://naturesnurtureblog.com/homemade-cleaning-wipes/

Citroner, G. (2020, April 14). The Best Materials to Make a Homemade Face Mask. Retrieved from https://www.healthline.com/health-news/the-best-material-for-a-homemade-face-mask#Quilters-cotton-performs-better-than-regular-cotton-

Coronavirus Disease 2019 (COVID-19) – Prevention & Treatment. (2020, May 5). Retrieved from https://www.cdc.gov/coronavirus/2019-ncov/prevent-getting-sick/prevention.html

Haven, P. (2018, August 7). 10 Ingredients to Avoid When Choosing Hand Sanitizer & Hand Soap... Retrieved from https://purehaven.com/10-ingredients-to-avoid-when-choosing-hand-sanitizer-hand-soap-for-back-to-school/

History of Virology. (2014, January 1). Retrieved from https://www.sciencedirect.com/science/article/pii/B9780128012383000787

How to Make Hand Sanitizer Using Just Two Ingredients. (2020, March 6). Retrieved from https://www.nbcchicago.com/news/coronavirus/how-to-make-hand-sanitizer-using-just-two-ingredients/2231894/

How to Put on and Remove a Face Mask . (2017, December 13). Retrieved from https://www.sfcdcp.org/communicable-disease/healthy-habits/how-to-put-on-and-remove-a-face-mask/

Medina, A. (2020, May 22). How long will it take to get a vaccine for COVID-19? Retrieved from https://www.ksat.com/news/local/2020/05/22/how-long-will-it-take-to-get-a-vaccine-for-covid-19/

O. (2018). 10 Types of viruses that are harmful to humans. Retrieved from https://enysuryo.blogspot.com/2011/09/10-types-of-viruses-that-are-harmful-to.html

Sampol, C. (2020, April 20). Surgical Masks, Respirators, Barrier Masks: Which Masks Actually Protect Against Coronavirus? Retrieved from http://emag.medicalexpo.com/which-masks-actually-protect-against-coronavirus/

Seladi-Schulman, J., PhD. (2020, April 22). How to Make a Face Mask with a Filter: Sew and No-Sew Instructions. Retrieved from https://www.healthline.com/health/how-to-make-a-face-mask-with-filter#no-sew-instructions

The Chemistry of Sanitizers: How They Protect Against the Coronavirus. (2019). Retrieved from https://info.noahtech.com/blog/the-chemistry-of-sanitizers-how-they-protect-against-the-coronavirus

When and how to use masks. (2020). Retrieved from https://www.who.int/emergencies/diseases/novel-coronavirus-2019/advice-for-public/when-and-how-to-use-masks#:%7E:text=If%20you%20are%20healthy%2C,dispose%20of%20it%20properly.

www.ingramcontent.com/pod-product-compliance
Lightning Source LLC
LaVergne TN
LVHW022050200926
848481LV00003B/851